Dear Rider,

In my previous two books, *Connected Riding®: An Introduction* and *Keys to Connection, Exercises for Riders*, I presented and illustrated the basic principles of Connected Riding. Familiarity with these concepts will enhance your understanding and speed your progress with Connected Groundwork.

In this volume, I share with you some of the secrets I have learned over the past 30 years—insights that have made a difference in the way I look at horses moving and how I can help them become better riding horses by working them from the ground. Effortless flying lead changes, smoother transitions, better lateral work and an all-around happier horse—one who is truly able to move forward—are just some of the results my students and I have seen time after time.

Tightness, bracing patterns, crookedness and on-the-forehand tendencies exist in all horses. Some have these patterns from birth. Others begin acquiring them as soon as halters are put on their heads, bits go in their mouths and riders get on their backs. The groundwork exercises in this book—which form the foundation of Connected Riding—have restored movement, function and elasticity to hundreds of horses. The following exercises will help you:

- Understand your horse's behavior and movement patterns
- Use your body more efficiently to facilitate response and change in your horse
- See and feel how you can help your horse develop his lifting and pushing muscles rather than his bracing and pulling muscles
- Assess what your horse needs *today*.

In addition, *Connected Groundwork I* will help your horse:

- Release tension and increase relaxation
- Enhance his focus, willingness and participation
- Prepare his muscles before being ridden
- Maintain his core muscle use when ridden and at rest
- Keep his back lifting and his engagement coming, and develop his "pushing power"
- Overcome bracing patterns and reduce stress that inhibit performance and learning
- Use both sides of his body with equal freedom
- Shift his weight in movement in three dimensions: front to back, side to side, down to up
- Reciprocate by taking connection and responsibility for carrying himself
- Achieve his full potential in freedom of movement.

Connected Groundwork exercises not only loosen, reeducate and strengthen your horse's body; they give you keen assessment tools that tell you a great deal about the state of your horse's mind and body—and how he is likely to respond under saddle each day.

It is my hope that this book will be the beginning of your journey toward true connection with your horse!

Peggy Cummings

Connected Groundwork I

Exercises for Developing and Maintaining Freedom of Movement and Self-Carriage

By Peggy Cummings

*Creator and Founder of
Connected Groundwork®
and Connected Riding®*

With Bobbie Lieberman

Photographs by Lynne Glazer

Connected Groundwork I
Exercises for Developing and Maintaining
Freedom of Movement and Self-Carriage
By Peggy Cummings with Bobbie Lieberman
Photographs by Lynne Glazer

ISBN # 0-9759217-0-3

© 2004 Peggy Cummings and Connected Enterprises, Inc.
All rights reserved. No part of this book may be used or reproduced in any manner without written permission of the publisher, except in the case of brief quotations included in a magazine, newspaper or website. Printed in the United States of America.

SAFETY DISCLAIMER
The author and publisher wish to remind the reader that horseback riding and horse-related activities are by their nature hazardous and can result in serious injuries because of a variety of related and/or unrelated reasons including, but not limited to, the fact that behavior—whether of people or horses—can be unpredictable. The reader is strongly encouraged and advised to assume responsibility for her or his own actions and personal safety by complying with all standard and other sensible equine safety procedures. Please, protect yourself by wearing a properly fitted and secured certified ASTM-SEI equestrian helmet and appropriate riding shoes with heels when you are riding or working around horses. At all times use your best sense and consideration when around horses and other riders. This book cannot replace the reader's own sound judgment and good decision-making nor can it disclose all of the potential hazards and/or risks the reader may encounter.

The material presented in this book has worked to the benefit of the author and her students. The sharing of this information is not a guarantee or promise of any results which you may or may not obtain. Although believing that her advice is sound and well founded, the author specifically states that neither she nor the publisher will be liable to anyone for damages caused by the reader's reliance upon any of the information contained in this book.

Cover design by Henne Schoemaker

Cover photo by Lynne Glazer

Book design by Bobbie Lieberman

To order additional copies, call 1-800-310-2192 or visit www.connectedriding.com

DEDICATION

I dedicate this book to Linda Tellington-Jones and her sister, Robyn Hood. Linda is the founder and creator of the Tellington Touch Equine Awareness Method (TTEAM™). Robyn is a master teacher and ambassador of TTEAM work worldwide. Their philosophy and techniques for working with horses and humans have been instrumental in the development of my work. We are kindred spirits with similar missions. I deeply respect their contribution of bridging human and animal understanding and cooperation.

ACKNOWLEDGEMENTS

This book represents a Connected labor of love, devotion and commitment from a team of people who support the work and mission of Connected Riding®. I am blessed and grateful for the wonderful community of people who share my vision of evolving the connection between horse and human.

The Groundwork book team—it does take a village:

Editor and wordsmith—Bobbie Jo Lieberman. Bobbie is my guide, mentor and creative friend for all of my writing projects. *kindredspiritRJL@earthlink.net*

Photographer extraordinaire—Lynne Glazer. Lynne took the fabulous photos that capture the essence of the groundwork. *www.lynnesite.com*

Additional editing and proofreading, giving countless hours to refining the text—Joan Thompson, Lindsay Cummings, Jillian Kreinbring, Sara Scribner, Karen Pelletreau, Helen Yee and Susan Cook.

Cover Design—Henne Schoemaker, *www.hennedesign.com*

Marketing—Kellie Lawless, *www.bluemoonmarketingstrategies.com*

Equine models and their people—Q (Celesteele) and Ember (Remember Me), Lynne Glazer; Marrukah Snow, Valerie Power; Perle, Bobbie Lieberman; and my own beloved equine companion of 23 years, Scotia.

Inspiration—Bobbie Jo Lieberman and her mare, Perle, Lynne Glazer and her gelding Q, and hundreds of unrelenting students requesting this book.

Technical support and master of the fine art of uploading—Scott Graham

Moral support, unending encouragement, holders of the vision—Susan Cook and Lana Daugherty.—*Peggy Cummings, Poulsbo, Wash., September 2004*

Note: Throughout this book, for simplicity riders and handlers are referred to as "she"; most horses are referred to as "he."

Connected Groundwork I

*Exercises for Developing and Maintaining
Freedom of Movement and Self-Carriage*

By Peggy Cummings with Bobbie Lieberman

Photographs by Lynne Glazer

Dear Rider. 2
Acknowledgements. 5
Introduction to Connected Groundwork 7
Posture is Everything (But it May Not Be What You Think it is). 10
Remember to Remember: Check in With Your Horse. 18
How to Use the Connected Groundwork Halter and Leadline. 20

Connected Groundwork I: Core Exercises

    Cheek Press. 24
    Cheek Delineation. 26
    Caterpillar. 28
    Chin Rest. 30
    Shoulder Delineation 32
    Shoulder Press. 33
    Heart-Girth Press. 35
    Wither Rock. 36
    Spine Roll. 38
    Spine Rake. 39
    The Fan. 40
    The Wave. 41
    Hip Press. 42
    Sacral Rock. 44
    Tail Rock. 46

Introduction to Connected Leading 47

    Tracing the Arc. 49
    Elephant's Trunk. 51
    Slide Up/Slide Out 53
    Combing the Line. 54
    Walking the S, One Hand. 55

The TTouch Pressure Scale 57
Glossary of Connected Groundwork Terms. 58
Quick Reference Guide. 60
Resources and Recommended Reading. 61
A Word from Peggy. 62

Introduction to Connected Groundwork

The purpose of Connected Groundwork is to develop the muscular, postural and movement patterns of self-carriage. For horses to be in self-carriage, they must be able to lift their musculoskeletal system from down to up, allowing them to shift their weight from side to side and from forehand to haunches while consistently releasing the poll and the base of the neck while moving forward. It is beneficial for horses to begin learning about these patterns of self-carriage before supporting the weight of a rider.

We have all seen horses react to flies on their body. Day after day they react to the same light minimal touch of the fly. Why, then, do they so easily tune out human beings? I frequently hear the following: " My horse is not listening to me." "My horse is lazy." "My horse is stubborn." And the list goes on. Horses tune out human beings or develop behavioral reactions when communication is not clear or they are handled in a way that throws them out of balance and disconnects them.

Disconnection: The Three C's (Compression, Counterbalancing, Compensation)
In a cycle of disconnection, movement cannot flow freely through the horse because parts of the horse's body are compressed. The rider works harder to try to create the desired movement and oftentimes becomes even more unbalanced. The horse then compensates by mechanically counterbalancing the rider's imbalance. This creates compensatory stress when parts of the horse's body are overtaxed from taking up the slack for inefficient movement. Disconnection results in more labored work and/or evasions as horse and rider remain in a persistently disconnected pattern.

Signs of Disconnection
- Bracing
- Compressing
- Unyielding
- Mechanical, stiff movement
- False frame
- Heavy on the forehand
- Evasive
- Unresponsive
- Overreactive

Ideally, during connection, a horse's movement travels up from the hind end through the human's body, moving out through the arms to the horse's front end. This movement then travels back through the horse's body and the cycle repeats. When a horse or human falls out of balance, connection can be re-established through Connected Riding's Rebalancing Cycle (see *Connected Riding: An Introduction*, p. 67-68).

Bracing Begets Bracing
During moments of tension or falling out of balance, horses and humans brace their bodies. When two beings move together while bracing, they lose their elasticity and ability to rebalance. The horse's quality of movement, his willingness and his desire to cooperate slip away. When balance is lost, more evasions and training issues, such as

spooking, tripping, shortened stride and running through the bridle take place.

When habitual bracing patterns occur, muscles clump together and tighten, losing their capacity for freedom of movement. In addition, muscle tightness places undue pressure on the skeletal system of the horse: bones move out of alignment, tension increases and movement cannot flow freely through the body. This out-of-balance posture keeps a horse heavy on the forehand. In the face of such imbalances, drilling with coercive or repetitive training methods, especially with gadgets like martingales and draw reins, forces horses into a false frame. Obedience may be achieved, but elasticity, resiliency and soundness are often compromised or lost.

Signs of Connection
- Releasing
- Expanding
- Balancing and rebalancing
- Movement with freedom and purpose
- Coming through
- Working from the hind end
- Reciprocity
- Partnership

Connection: Releasing, Expanding, Balancing
On the other hand, when horses are coming through and moving freely without bracing, there is an oscillating, sequential movement through the spine, like that of the caterpillar. Horse and caterpillar movement follow a constant and sequential pattern of releasing and re-engaging. When horses exhibit bracing patterns, it is as if several of their segments are stuck together; freedom of movement is lost.

Most horses who are ridden become stiffer by the year even though they may have loving humans who care for them. Many riders unintentionally contribute to their horse's bracing patterns. However, by making subtle changes in the way they use their bodies when they ride and handle their horses, riders can regain their horse's suppleness. Such changes completely shift the way horses move, learn and respond. With the aid of Connected Groundwork, bracing patterns in horse and human can be broken and connection rediscovered.

From Disconnection to Connection
Moving from patterns of disconnection to connection results in communication between horse and rider that travels from body to body and mind to mind, inviting reciprocity, observation, response and responsibility in both horse and rider. In order for this transformation to occur, the following are necessary:

- The rider must pay attention to her body.
- Every time there is bracing in the horse or human, it needs to be released.
- Every evasion needs to be observed as an out-of-balance, on-the-forehand situation that can be changed by shifting the horse's center of balance back toward the haunches.
- The horse's body needs to have the freedom to move like a Slinky™ without kinks, so he can constantly shift weight in three dimensions—front to back, side to side, and down to up.

Connected Groundwork I: Exercises for Developing and Maintaining
Freedom of Movement and Self-Carriage
© 2004 Connected Enterprises, Inc.
By Peggy Cummings with photographs by Lynne Glazer
Call 1-800-310-2192 or visit www.peggycummings.com

So why isn't everybody riding and handling horses in connection? Because we often fall into habitual, unconscious movement patterns that are ineffective ways of using our bodies. Over time, compensatory patterns emerge, and inefficient movement creates more restricted movement in both horse and rider.

First Step to Connection: Awareness
Most riders are willing to learn and are truly interested in doing the best for their horses. One of the ways to achieve the best for the horse is by increasing rider/handler awareness. This includes the following:

- Having a clear picture of the desired result
- Knowing what is working
- Knowing what is not working and how to change it
- Willingness to change when something is not working.

Riders must also learn to change long-held habits and adopt new methods in order to move from:

- Bracing to releasing
- Holding to supporting
- Squeezing to alternating rhythmical movement
- Reacting to thinking
- Demanding to asking
- Repetitive drilling to "chunking" the exercise into small segments.

By using the principles of Connected Groundwork and Connected Riding with thousands of horses and riders, I have witnessed the instantaneous change from compressed, choppy, flat movement to animated, light, suspended gaits. Horses and riders achieve movements and goals they never thought possible. The change is miraculous. The rules are simple. The shift is immediate—as long as you are aware.

Every horse and rider has the possibility of creating a new cycle of lightening, expanding, releasing and reopening with every stride. If you take just ten to 15 minutes each day to learn and practice the exercises in this book, your increments of ease will increase until your riding becomes a continuous string of magical, connected strides.

> **Note**: Although most of the exercises in this book are shown from the left side of the horse for consistency, be sure to do them from both sides. The exercises are presented in a logical learning sequence for both you and your horse, although you can initiate any exercise from either side and do them in any order.

Connected Groundwork I: Exercises for Developing and Maintaining
Freedom of Movement and Self-Carriage
© 2004 Connected Enterprises, Inc.
By Peggy Cummings with photographs by Lynne Glazer
Call 1-800-310-2192 or visit www.connectedriding.com

Posture is Everything
(But it May Not Be What You Think)

Fire the posture police and learn the feeling of alignment within yourself. This is the most important foundation for your success with Connected Groundwork.

Your posture and how you use your body are of the utmost importance in doing groundwork effectively. When you do groundwork, you must be able to recognize when you are in *neutral pelvis* and remember to return there consistently. Neutral pelvis is the position in which the body rebalances naturally, allows the core muscles to engage and the limbs to move independently. When you are not in neutral pelvis, your communication is not clear, your body feels like dead weight to your horse, and he is forced to carry you by bracing. Riders in neutral pelvis create a cycle of lightening, expanding, releasing and reopening with each stride of the horse. (For more information on how to establish the feeling of neutral pelvis, refer to the exercises in *Connected Riding: An Introduction*, p. 34-36, and *Keys to Connection: Exercises for Riders*, Keys 1-4.)

A horse can tell immediately when his handler is in neutral pelvis because he feels a sequential oscillating rhythm through the lines and halter. This rhythm invites him to participate by releasing tension and bracing patterns. All horses move more efficiently when their muscles are warmed up without tension. The habits that Connected Riding develops in horses allow efficient movement and rebalancing with minimal or no bracing. It is a continuous process of remembering to remember.

Are you aware of your own **unconscious habits** when it comes to your posture? Many of us stand in dysfunctional ways and rigidly brace to counterbalance ourselves. Our bodies are designed to readjust and rebalance our weight so we remain upright. If we do not release and rebalance but situate ourselves in static positions, our stiffness and tightness will be transmitted to our horses. The first step towards releasing and rebalancing is to recognize our own unconscious postural habits and patterns.

Poor posture in the rider (right) leads to counterbalancing, stiffness and bracing in both horse and rider.

Connected Groundwork I: Exercises for Developing and Maintaining
Freedom of Movement and Self-Carriage
© 2004 Connected Enterprises, Inc.
By Peggy Cummings with photographs by Lynne Glazer
Call 1-800-310-2192 or visit www.connectedriding.com

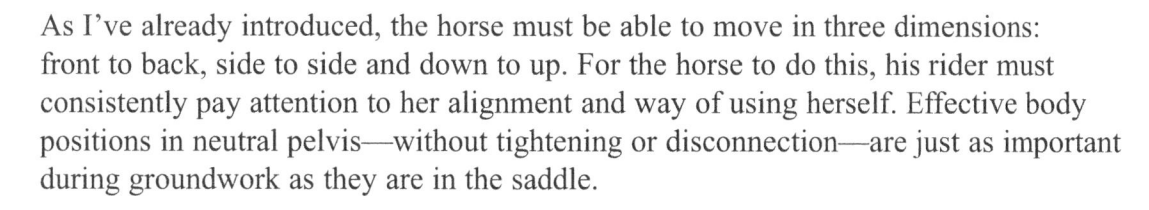

As I've already introduced, the horse must be able to move in three dimensions: front to back, side to side and down to up. For the horse to do this, his rider must consistently pay attention to her alignment and way of using herself. Effective body positions in neutral pelvis—without tightening or disconnection—are just as important during groundwork as they are in the saddle.

Core muscles such as the rectus abdominus and latissimus dorsi maintain the body's uprightness. When the rider is in neutral pelvis, these muscles engage automatically to maintain balance in any type of situation. A rider in neutral pelvis can meet resistance, such as a sudden spook or a horse's shoulder falling in on a circle, with freedom and stability. In Connected Groundwork, the rider's core muscles must also be engaged and active, so that the horse can move freely.

As you learn to work with your horse without tightness, you will engage your core muscles, adding tiny oscillations and torso rotations (see *Keys to Connection, Exercises for Riders*, Rotation, Keys 1 and 2), which increase the clarity of the message the horse receives through the halter and lines. The horse's natural tendency toward fight-or-flight diminishes when clear communication is established between horse and human. Thus, clear communication enhances trust and reciprocity.

The following exercises are useful in achieving neutral pelvis and taking stress out of your back when riding or working around your horse:

1) FINDING NEUTRAL PELVIS (YOUR MIDDLE) ON THE EDGE OF A CHAIR

The purpose of this exercise is to help riders recognize the contrasts between the *Arched, Slumped* and *Neutral* postures. Sit on the edge of the chair and experiment doing a very tiny movement of "buoying" your upper body back and forth. If you raise your sternum

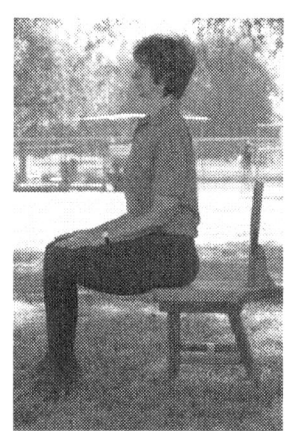

ARCHED   **NEUTRAL**   **SLUMPED**

slightly, what happens to the tiny movement? Does the buoying take more effort (i.e., is the back and forth movement even or jerky)? If you drop your sternum slightly, what happens to the movement? How does this back and forth movement differ from the movement when you lift the sternum? Which posture allows you to move with most

---

Connected Groundwork I: Exercises for Developing and Maintaining
Freedom of Movement and Self-Carriage
© 2004 Connected Enterprises, Inc.
By Peggy Cummings with photographs by Lynne Glazer
Call 1-800-310-2192 or visit www.peggycummings.com

ease? Notice how it feels when the movement is so subtle that it would hardly be visible if someone were watching.

When you have found the place where the movement takes the least effort, seems the easiest to maintain and is even, then chances are you have found your middle. Now place one hand on your sternum, palm against your body. Place the other hand on your sacrum, palm away from your body. Gently pulse your hands in three or four light presses. Does the pressing feel even and springy in both places? Then, slightly arch your back by lifting the sternum and repeat the light presses. Is your front hand springier than the back hand? Now, slightly slump by dropping the sternum and repeat the light presses. Is your back hand springier than your front hand? Return to the place where your hands feel evenly springy and you will be in the middle.

Arching/Hollowing 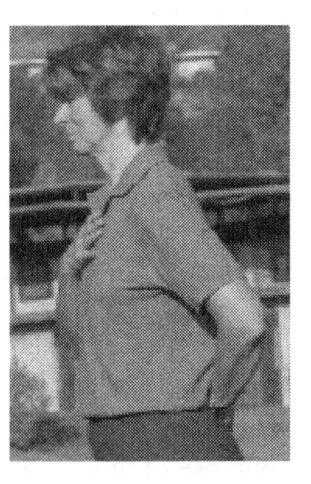
Now you have established a contrast between arching, middle and slumping. Try this exercise for an awareness of how you use your back. With your eyes closed and your hands on the sternum and sacrum, find your middle. Slowly begin lifting the sternum and feel the change under your hands and in your lower back. Now slowly release inside your body and let the sternum return to where you just started this exercise. Do this exercise two or three times very slowly and notice the relationship between your sternum and the sacrum. Now repeat this with your back hand higher, just above your waist; feel when the back hollows and when it feels flatter and fuller. If your habit is to arch/hollow your back when sitting on the horse or when stressing and bracing, remember the feeling of releasing in your body and letting the back fill and flatten. Practice the sensation of letting go and softening in the lower back area repeatedly to override the habit of hollowing and tensing unconsciously.

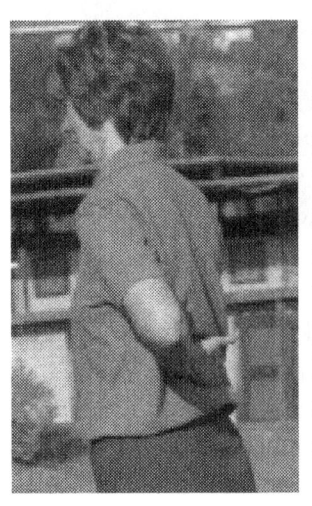

Slumping/Collapsing
Again, with your eyes closed and standing or sitting in the middle, place your hands on your sternum and sacrum. Slowly drop the sternum less than an inch and feel the change under your hands in the lower back. Repeat two or three times very slowly and notice the relationship between the sternum and sacrum. Now repeat this with your back hand just above the waist, always slowly returning your sacrum to the place where you began the exercise. Notice that when you slump, your lower back is rounder, and when you slowly open the ribcage and increase the distance between your belly button and sternum, you can return to the place where you began the exercise.

Connected Groundwork I: Exercises for Developing and Maintaining
Freedom of Movement and Self-Carriage
© 2004 Connected Enterprises, Inc.
By Peggy Cummings with photographs by Lynne Glazer
Call 1-800-310-2192 or visit www.connectedriding.com

If your habit is to drop the sternum in stress or unconscious posture, remember the feeling of slowly opening the ribcage and lengthening between the sternum and belly button. Remember to open your ribcage when your reaction is to collapse or slump.

Now experiment with moving your thighs as if you were alternately moving your knees back towards your hips. The movement feels like peddling a unicycle backwards. It involves engaging the thigh muscles; when you are in neutral pelvis, this movement is very easy and feels as if the bones slide easily inside your skin. When you lift or drop the sternum, your movement loses its ease and subtlety. Neutral pelvis is the only place where your arms and legs have independent movement from your torso.

2) CHECKING FOR NEUTRAL PELVIS, SITTING, Exercise 1

ARCHED   **NEUTRAL**   **SLUMPED**

A way to check your neutral pelvis position is to turn the chair around and straddle it. Then, make a fist and press against the back of the chair. When you are in neutral pelvis, pressing on the back of the chair will feel like an even press, and your body will stay soft. This is the way your body needs to feel when you are doing Connected Groundwork exercises such as *Shoulder Press*. The spine feels as if it lengthens and the back stays soft; there will be no need for bracing. It feels like the press of your hand goes through to your seat bones; you will feel deeper and more solid in the chair without adding any effort. If you slightly lift your sternum, the press will feel more like a push. The push will send your body backwards unless you brace against the push. The push of your hand does not go through to your seat and you may feel some discomfort in your lower back. If you slightly lower the sternum, the press against the chair also becomes a push. Your upper body will feel unstable because there is no connection through from your hand to your seat bones.

Building Awareness and Re-educating the Body Through Movement

Practicing these exercises will help you to increase your awareness of your movement habits. You will also practice non-habitual movement to re-educate your body. Moshe Feldenkrais, an Israeli physicist and movement expert who created the Feldenkrais Method®, stated "The nervous system can learn and change patterns through simple exercises of non-habitual movement that do not cause fear or pain." This kind of non-habitual movement is necessary to quietly establish new information in you and your horse's neural pathways. It allows you both to release old patterns of holding and habitual posture in order to feel and allow a broader, freer range of motion and establish new, effective movement patterns.

Connected Groundwork I: Exercises for Developing and Maintaining Freedom of Movement and Self-Carriage
© 2004 Connected Enterprises, Inc.
By Peggy Cummings with photographs by Lynne Glazer
Call 1-800-310-2192 or visit www.peggycummings.com

3) CHECKING FOR NEUTRAL PELVIS, SITTING, Exercise 2

Similar results are achieved when you hold the back of the chair and stretch back from your elbows. The upper body will be unstable unless you are in neutral pelvis. When you take contact on the chair and are out of balance, you may feel pulled forward unless you brace, in which case you will go backwards. When you are in neutral pelvis, the contact feels stable and supportive. This is the way the contact on the halter and line needs to feel when you are doing Connected Groundwork exercises.

ARCHED   NEUTRAL   SLUMPED

The subtle movement of the legs is only simple and minute when you are in neutral pelvis. The feeling of stability in your arms and elbows when you are in neutral is the connection I refer to as "Owning Your Elbows" (see *Glossary, p.58*).

These exercises are important because biomechanically, when you are in neutral pelvis, both you and your horse can move without restriction. This empowers you to support and enhance your horse's natural movement. It is the place where all of your joints are moving and your upper body is subtly buoyed by the horse's motion. In this neutral pelvis posture, you are the most stable, and the strength of your stability helps override loss of balance in the horse. In addition, your ability to recover your balance is much quicker. You will become accustomed to the feeling of rebalancing, releasing tension and allowing the horse's movement to move through you whether you are working from the ground or under saddle.

4) FINDING YOUR NEUTRAL PELVIS (THE MIDDLE) WHILE STANDING

After you have familiarized yourself with finding the middle in the chair, stand with your feet about shoulder-width apart. Remember the sensation of the middle when you were sitting and notice if your tendency while standing is for your back to be slightly hollow, flat or slightly rounded. Repeat everything you did above except for the buoying. Then experiment with the sensation of your legs moving alternately (almost imperceptibly) as if your feet were in squishy mud. When you are in the middle, it feels as if the bones move easily inside your legs. When you are arching or slumping, the movement takes more effort and is not as subtle.

Connected Groundwork I: Exercises for Developing and Maintaining
Freedom of Movement and Self-Carriage
© 2004 Connected Enterprises, Inc.
By Peggy Cummings with photographs by Lynne Glazer
Call 1-800-310-2192 or visit www.connectedriding.com

It is very important when you stand to remember to unlock your knees. Close your eyes and lock your knees and then unlock them. What effect does that have on your upper body? Does it have an effect on your lower back? Locking your knees—as shown in the *arched* photo at right—not only affects your lower back and upper body, it also tightens the muscles in front of the hip joint, thereby adding stress to the hip flexors and pelvic muscles.

Opening (bending at) the hip
Begin by first finding the front of the hip joint by placing the heel of your hand on your hip bones with your fingers locating the crease between your torso and the top of your thigh. Place your fingertips in the fold that occurs when you lift your knee up. The point that you need to

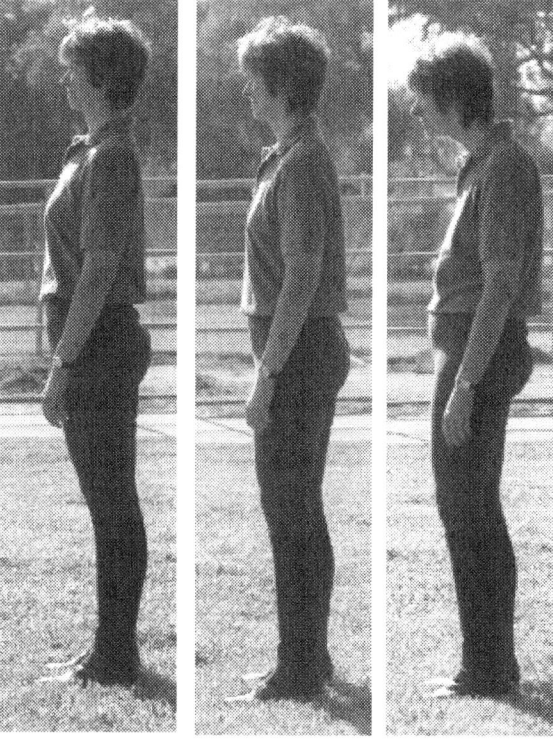

ARCHED   NEUTRAL   SLUMPED

find is closer to the midline of your body and when you press inward as your knee is raised, there will be a spot where one finger goes in deeper than all the rest. This is the spot that needs to remain soft without bracing. But it can only happen when your knees are soft and your upper body has no tension and is in the middle. If you point your fingers in towards that spot and lock your knees, you will notice that the one finger in each hand that could go deeper gets pushed out. When you unlock the knees, the finger has a place to go.

Learning to distinguish the sensation of when this area is tight and when it is soft is very important. This new awareness takes practice and remembering to remember to release tension. Most people, when they are standing, are habitually locked on one or both sides. Most of us have never been taught how or what to soften, what it is supposed to feel like when we are dynamically balanced and how to rebalance when we go into old habits of bracing and standing in a counterbalanced position. The familiar "Stand up straight and get your shoulders back" does not provide ease to our bodies nor does it tell us how to balance.

Connected Groundwork I: Exercises for Developing and Maintaining
Freedom of Movement and Self-Carriage
© 2004 Connected Enterprises, Inc.
By Peggy Cummings with photographs by Lynne Glazer
Call 1-800-310-2192 or visit www.peggycummings.com

ARCHED    **NEUTRAL**    **SLUMPED**

5) CHECKING FOR NEUTRAL PELVIS, STANDING

Stand facing the back of a chair. Stand close enough to put your fingertips on the back of the chair without reaching. Press lightly on the back of the chair and notice the differences in the three postures.

• When you are in neutral pelvis pressing on the back of a chair, the contact of your hands will feel firm and soft. There will be no stress anywhere in your body and you can move your legs minutely with ease as though you were moving your feet in squishy mud. The weight on your feet is evenly distributed and you can feel the press in the soles of your feet. Your position feels stable.

• When you are arched, the press on the back of the chair feels more like a push. There is stress in your upper body and lower back. The small movement of your legs feels forced. The weight on your feet is on your heels and the press from your hands cannot be felt in your feet. Your position is not stable.

• When you are slumped, the press on the chair is also a push. There is stress in your upper body as well as through your hips and upper thighs. The small movement in your legs is awkward. The weight on your feet is in your heels and the press from your hands does not go into your feet. Your position is not stable.

Connected Groundwork I: Exercises for Developing and Maintaining
Freedom of Movement and Self-Carriage
© 2004 Connected Enterprises, Inc.
By Peggy Cummings with photographs by Lynne Glazer
Call 1-800-310-2192 or visit www.connectedriding.com

Remember to Remember...

Reminders for standing in neutral pelvis:

• Find the middle in your upper body.

• Unlock your knees.

• Release your hip joints.

• Do minute movements with your legs as if you were marching in squishy mud; the thighs move imperceptibly. In other words, you feel as if you are moving bones inside your skin, and movement is barely perceptible to an onlooker. Make sure your entire foot remains on the ground as you move your legs.

• If your tendency is to arch your back in stress or standing, then you have to know what it feels like to release your back and let your upper body float one degree forward of the plumb line—an imaginary vertical line that runs perpendicular to the ground.

• If your tendency is to slump or collapse the sternum, you need to know what it feels like to open the ribcage and lengthen the distance between your navel and the bottom of the sternum.

REMEMBER TO REMEMBER:
Check in With Your Horse

Watching your horse before, during and after each exercise is *immensely important*. This work is about really knowing your horse and learning to observe and take note of his physical and mental changes. This is also a journey of self-reflection. Pay attention to how you use your body, how you are able to recognize and change habits and how you can integrate new information into your daily routines. Practice various Connected Groundwork exercises while walking your horse to and from the barn and while grooming. Apply two or three of these exercises before and after you ride. Notice the changes. Vary your daily routines, and do some exploring to find the exercises your horse prefers. When something becomes difficult for your horse, find a way to simplify it and gradually return to what was more challenging.

Notice the following in yourself:

- Are your knees unlocked?
- Are your hips released and centered over your seat bones?
- Is your lower back full and soft?
- Is your torso free to move from the hips?
- Are your elbows stretchy and elastic?
- Are your hands soft on the line?
- Are you breathing from your belly?

Notice the following in your horse as you lead him:

- What is the quality of his walk—alive, hyper or dull?
- Is his head up, down or level with the withers?
- Does his head go up when you start walking?
- Does his head go up when you stop walking?
- Is his head heavy in your hand?
- Is it difficult for him to maintain contact on the line?
- Is he pulling from the front or pushing from behind?
- Is he focused, distracted or shut down?
- Is he dragging any of his feet or uneven in his walk?

Signs of Connection:
Licking, chewing, deep breathing, yawning, eyes softening, blowing through the nostrils, nostrils flaring, mouth relaxing, head dropping, neck stretching or telescoping, push coming from the hind legs, back coming up, base of neck softening, stopping and starting easily, changing direction without stiffening, bracing or change of pace. The horse is with you, relaxed and focused.

Connected Groundwork I: Exercises for Developing and Maintaining
Freedom of Movement and Self-Carriage
© 2004 Connected Enterprises, Inc.
By Peggy Cummings with photographs by Lynne Glazer
Call 1-800-310-2192 or visit www.connectedriding.com

Signs of Disconnection:
Lack of focus, head high or neck too curled, bracing anywhere in the body, stiffening in transitions or when changing direction, head going up in transitions or when changing direction, suddenly changing tempo, backing up when starting an exercise, tripping, dragging the feet, spooking, fear of going through or over things, exhibiting crabbiness, nipping or biting, not wanting to be touched.

If your horse is showing signs of disconnection throughout an exercise and you proceed to another exercise, it does not mean that you are "letting the horse get away with something" or that he has not learned anything. On the contrary, the horse will probably surprise you with the amount of information he has processed. Do the exercise 10 minutes later or the next day. These breaks give your horse time to process and honor his way of learning. The only time an exercise is not integrated at some level is when a horse has a physical handicap or injury. Remember to be patient and observant. Most of all, enjoy the process!

DISCONNECTED   **CONNECTED**

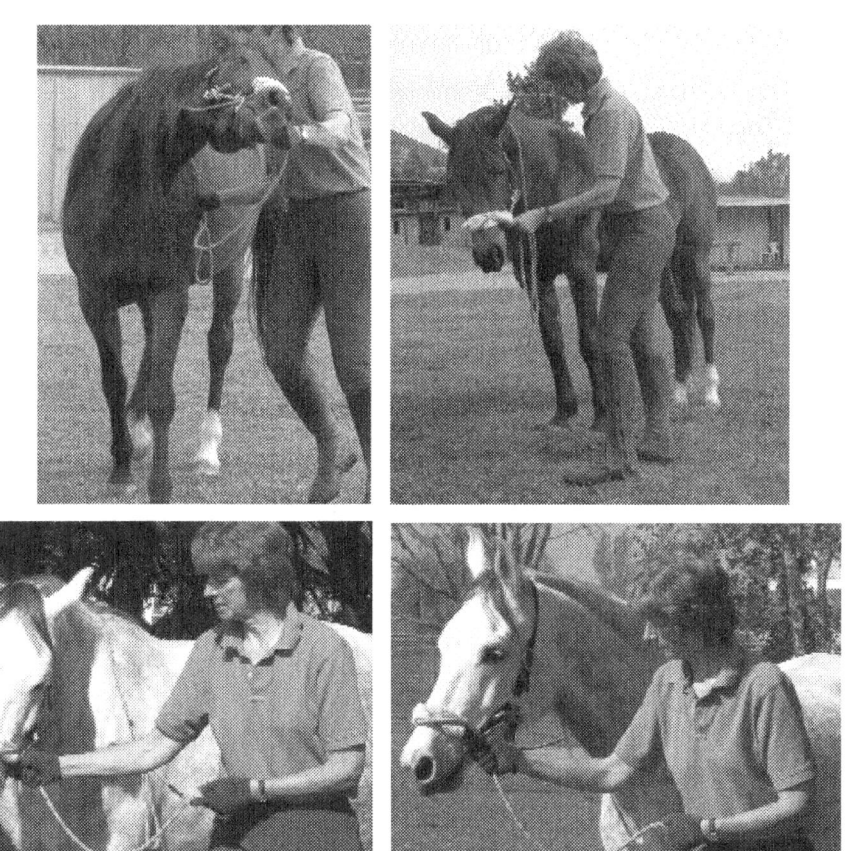

Here are two examples of disconnection followed by the horse softening, releasing and accepting. For further information, see **Shoulder Press** (p. 33) and **Walking the S, One Hand** (p. 55).

Connected Groundwork I: Exercises for Developing and Maintaining Freedom of Movement and Self-Carriage
© 2004 Connected Enterprises, Inc.
By Peggy Cummings with photographs by Lynne Glazer
Call 1-800-310-2192 or visit www.connectedriding.com

USING THE CONNECTED GROUNDWORK HALTER AND LINES

Have you ever experienced leading a horse and felt him brace and "stick," as if he can't move in one direction? Have you ever been leading a horse who consistently bends the opposite way that you are going? How about leading a horse who raises his head each time you start or stop walking?

When a horse moves, his head naturally has the ability to move up and down and from side to side. Many horses lose the side-to-side movement from unconscious habits of riders and trainers who compress or brace their bodies while riding or working with the horse on the ground. A horse may also be predisposed from birth to some lack of flexion in his body. Later in his life, riders who pull on his head, hang on his mouth or push him around contribute to his limited flexibility. Further damage occurs to any horse if we force him into postures using mechanical aids. He inevitably loses elasticity, flexibility and even soundness.

Connected Groundwork Halter and Lines facilitate Connected Leading.

We tend to lead horses from the left side. Horses—just like people—are more dominant on one side. Horses become primarily one-sided due to our leading habits. Often, the horse's left cheek and shoulder brace while he is being led. The horse will have a tendency to plant his left leg, and his head will go up and away from the handler during groundwork. This happens especially if the lead line is attached under the chin and the handler pulls on it. The resulting loss of lateral flexion is made worse by unconscious mounting habits. When a rider mounts with tightness in the back and grabs the back of the saddle, the horse braces his left shoulder and offsets his head to the right to compensate for the dead weight pulling up onto his back. All of these habits deliver negative input into our horses' bodies and contribute to bracing and compression patterns.

These scenarios inspired me to develop the Connected Groundwork halter, a design that supports a horse's head and enables free movement. Freedom of the head allows the horse's movement patterns to be reeducated with groundwork exercises. In creating Connected Groundwork, my goal was to find a way to help horses reestablish the walk, the gait that loses the most impulsion and energy from compressive riding and training habits. When the walk has no swing, the horse's head braces at the poll, the base of the neck is stuck and there is no lift in the back, shifting of weight from side to side, or pushing power from the hind legs.

Connected Groundwork I: Exercises for Developing and Maintaining
Freedom of Movement and Self-Carriage
© 2004 Connected Enterprises, Inc.
By Peggy Cummings with photographs by Lynne Glazer
Call 1-800-310-2192 or visit www.connectedriding.com

What remains when the walk doesn't swing is an up-and-down, bobbing, bracing movement. The head and neck stop telescoping forward, up and out, and instead retract back (down and in) toward the horse's body. In addition, the subtle side-to-side oscillation of the horse's head is lost.

Design of the Groundwork Halter
When I first began developing the Connected Groundwork system, I used a TTEAM soft lead or chain lead laced through the halter to create a snug contact that communicated a clear message when I moved the horse's head. But I found there were times when even the snugged-up halter would slip on the offside either up to or into the horse's eye. Because I wanted a very minute differentiation of movement of the head, the halters were still not snug enough to give subtle, clear messages so that the handler's contact would transmit slow, fine directional movements.

When I first discovered the importance of the groundwork exercises, my frustration grew because most of the horses I worked with in clinics were not wearing well-fitting halters. They did not fit the horse's heads snugly enough (even with a line laced through them) to transmit the subtle messages necessary for fine motor movements. These concerns led me to create a new halter for my groundwork exercises. With the help of Nancy Camp, illustrator of *Connected Riding, An Introduction* and *Keys to Connection, Exercises for Riders* and a student and teacher of Connected Riding, I developed a prototype that evolved to become the halter we now use.

A correctly fitted halter and line are necessary to achieve light, precise movements that help your horse override tendencies to brace or "stick" in response to contact.

What is useful and unique about this halter?

- It is very adjustable (in three places) to fit many horse's heads snugly.
- It does not slip and slide across the face and is gentle to the horse's nose with its fleece lining.
- It allows the handler to use very light and precise movements that are readily felt by the horse.
- There is no chin hook underneath but rather rings on each side. A line run through these side rings gives the horse much clearer messages of what you intend.

When a halter is loose on the horse's head and someone is doing the subtle Connected Groundwork movements, more resistance is actually created because the horse feels the contact as unclear, jerky and harsh. The Connected Groundwork halter allows the handler to support the head with lightness while maintaining a clear connection.

The goal of the groundwork is to communicate clear, quiet differentiation of movement to the horse. What I appreciate about the groundwork halter is the way it allows a light hand to transmit a message, without pushing, pulling or grabbing. However, even with this halter, old handling habits of "doing," pushing, pulling and yanking on the lead line may still occur. The handler must change her focus and intention. So, remember to breathe, release your back, lighten your arm and soften in your hip joints and knees. Have fun remembering to remember!

Design of the Groundwork Lines
As mentioned earlier, originally I used the TTEAM soft lead instead of a standard lead rope. These leadlines can allow oscillation of the poll and encourage a horse to telescope his head and neck into contact. But I needed more length than the soft lead allowed and less bulk than a longe line. Also, the line needed to be a certain diameter that was not too thick or thin, to allow holding the loops in my hand, and not so smooth that it slipped. The line also needed to have a slight stretch and "give", and be the right texture to allow my hand to slide up and down without dropping the connection to the horse. Most importantly, the lines had to be threaded up through the halter to give the horse the support of a snug harness so the head could oscillate and release with ease. I did not want a lead with a snap hooked on to the side because the snap could wiggle and interrupt the connection at a time the horse needs uninterrupted support and contact.

I strongly recommend the use of well-fitting **gloves** as you do the groundwork, especially while your hands are sliding up or out on the line. Gloves will keep your hands soft and prevent chafing. Should a horse become momentarily startled, I usually release the line and then take the slack back up.

The series of photos on the following page demonstrate the method of threading the line through the halter on one or both sides.

> **Remember to Remember**
> Because the halter must be snug in order to function properly, loosen and readjust your halter each time you use it by opening the buckle under the noseband.

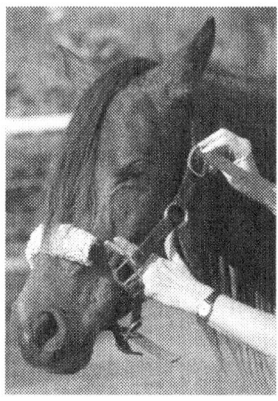

1. Adjust the crownpiece so that the noseband is 1 1/2 to 2 fingers below the base of the cheekbone.

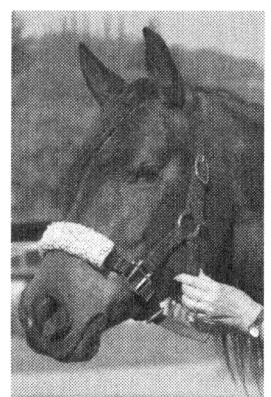

2. Adjust the cheekpiece so that it fits snugly. This keeps the halter from sliding from side to side.

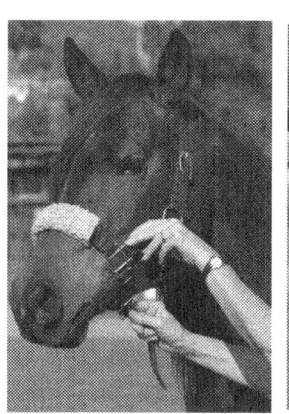

3. Adjust the noseband so that it is snug, allowing you to move the head with great precision.

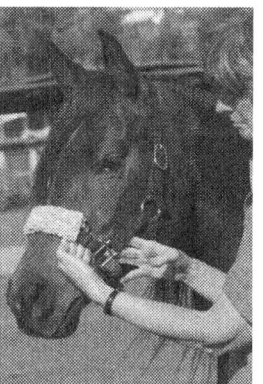

4. A well-adjusted halter still has room for you to slip your fingers beneath the noseband and cheekpiece.

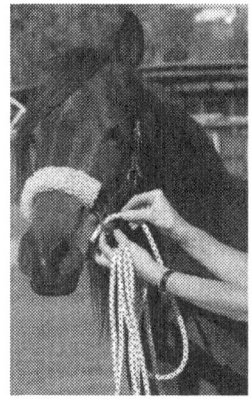

5. Weaving the line through the halter: Insert the line through the bottom ring from the outside in and down.

6. Bring the line over the top of the noseband in preparation for threading it back through the bottom ring...

7. Thread the tip of the line from the inside to the outside of the bottom ring...

8. ....and pull it through so that you have enough line to go up to the top ring to tie a slip knot.

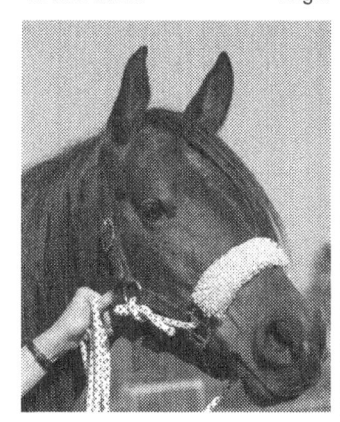

9. Slip the end of the line from the inside to the outside at the top ring, and tie a slip knot.

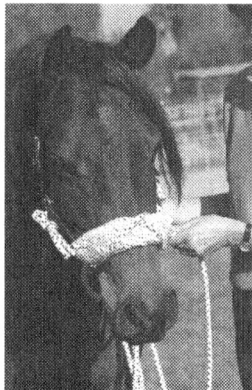

10. Repeat on the other side. The two lines form an "X" over the nose. Be sure that the crossover point is centered on the noseband.

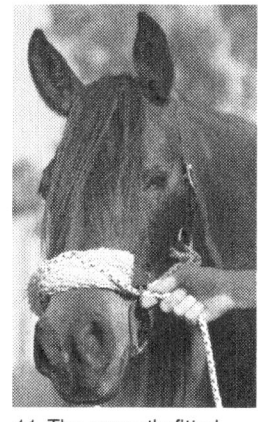

11. The correctly fitted Connected Groundwork halter and line enables you to maintain a snug contact without pulling on the horse's head.

Note:
Fitting the groundwork lines from both sides of the halter as shown enables you to switch sides easily without stopping to reconfigure your equipment.

Connected Groundwork I: Exercises for Developing and Maintaining
Freedom of Movement and Self-Carriage
© 2004 Connected Enterprises, Inc.
By Peggy Cummings with photographs by Lynne Glazer
Call 1-800-310-2192 or visit www.connectedriding.com

CHEEK PRESS

PURPOSE: *Cheek Press* assesses the ability of the horse to release and rotate his head one or two degrees in each direction. It gives you a chance to observe if he is relaxing or holding in the poll. If the horse cannot give in this area, he will not be able to release throughout the rest of his body, bend, lift his back or come through.

PROCEDURE: Stand on the left side of the horse's head facing the throatlatch. Place your left hand on the bridge of the nose across the noseband. Make a loose fist with your right hand and place it in the center of the cheek. *Make sure your wrist is straight to maintain connection with the horse.* The front hand invites the head to come towards you, and the back hand suggests that the cheek move away from you. Stand a few seconds with 1 or 2 degrees of pressure, allowing the horse to accept your hands (see p. 57 for *TTouch pressure scale*). Then add 2 to 4 degrees of pressure and wait. You are asking the horse's head to soften and yield slightly to the side. The hand on the nose feels as if you are bringing the head towards you while the hand on the cheek counterbalances while pressing away. Take a deep breath and stay there for five seconds. *Slowly* increase the pressure on the cheek and nose from 3 to 5 degrees. Take another breath

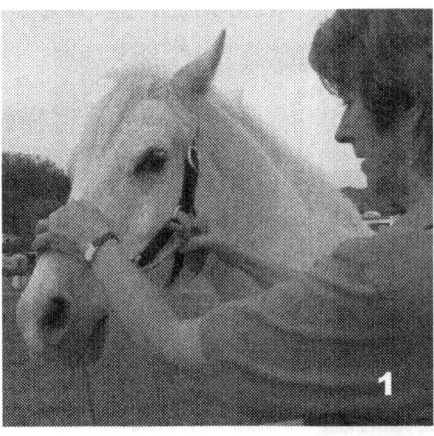

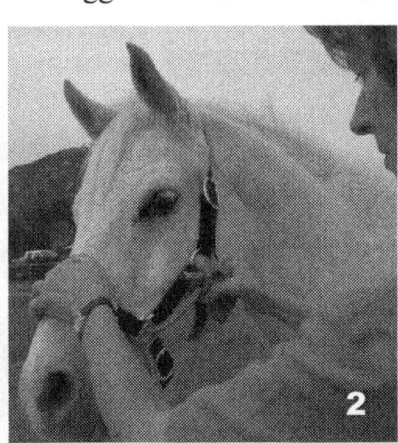

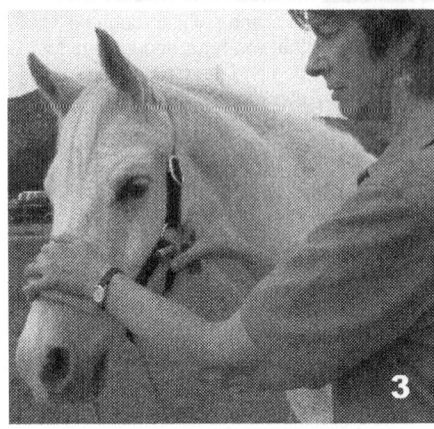

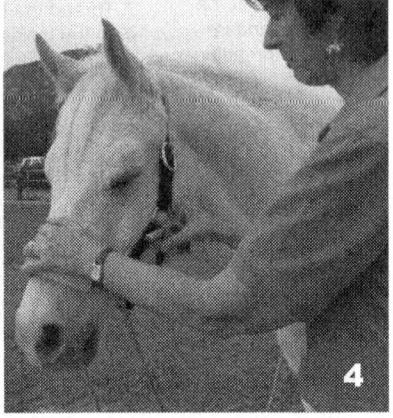

Photo 1: "I'm not so sure I want your hands on my face!"
Photo 2: "I'm thinking...this might not be quite so bad."
Photo 3: "*Hmmmmm......*maybe you've got something there."
Photo 4: "*Aaaah.....*I appreciate the way my head feels relaxed and supported."

Connected Groundwork I: Exercises for Developing and Maintaining
Freedom of Movement and Self-Carriage
© 2004 Connected Enterprises, Inc.
By Peggy Cummings with photographs by Lynne Glazer
Call 1-800-310-2192 or visit www.connectedriding.com

and stay there for a few seconds. Slowly release the pressure on the cheek, take your hands off the horse and observe him quietly for 20 seconds or more. Repeat the exercise two to four times. **Rather than forcing the movement, the key is to give the horse the *suggestion* of movement and then allow him to willingly yield.**

OBSERVATIONS: Notice if the horse is more flexible on one side or the other. Learn to recognize what bracing patterns the horse exhibits that day. For instance when you place your hands on the horse's face, does the horse:

- Brace and continue to brace?
- Brace and then melt (soften)?
- Melt upon connection?

As the horse releases, you may feel the head soften under your hands or the cheek yield under your fist. The head may drop, the eyes may start to close, their look may soften. The nostrils sometimes flare or the horse can take a big breath. Occasionally the horse will shake his head and neck or entire body and let out a big snort. Sometimes their mouths seems to tremble, their whiskers wiggle or their nose will drip. Oftentimes nothing happens until you take your hands away, and then any of the aforementioned signs may occur.

When a horse is bracing, he may not even want your hands on his nose and cheek. Sometimes as you increase pressure on the cheek, the horse will pull away, raise his head or plunge it downward. Other times, horses will start backing up as you put your hands on their faces or they start backing when you begin to press. These are all signs of bracing and extreme tightness, or they may indicate temporomandibular joint (TMJ), dental or chiropractic issues in the neck.

If the horse does not release or his response is really intense, give him time to think about the exercise by going on a two-minute walk, moving on to another exercise or trying again on another day. Later, even though the horse seemed averse to the exercise, the horse may drop his head or you might observe other signs of releasing. Do a different exercise such as *Cheek Delineation,* or try *Cheek Press* on the other side and see what the response is. Another option is to proceed with other exercises and before you finish, come back and do *Cheek Press* again. I have always found a positive change in this circumstance except with horses who have major dental imbalances or simply don't want their heads touched.

If the horse is stiffer on one side, the shoulder on that same side will also be tighter as will the base of the neck and the area part way up the neck near the fourth cervical vertebra.

Connected Groundwork I: Exercises for Developing and Maintaining
Freedom of Movement and Self-Carriage
© 2004 Connected Enterprises, Inc.
By Peggy Cummings with photographs by Lynne Glazer
Call 1-800-310-2192 or visit www.connectedriding.com

CHEEK DELINEATION

PURPOSE:
Cheek Delineation is another poll-releasing exercise to improve the mobility and flexibility in the area of the poll (atlas and axis joints) and to ensure that lateral rotation to both sides is equal.

PROCEDURE:
Stand on the left side of the horse facing his throatlatch area. Place your left hand on the bridge of the horse's nose across the noseband or on the line snugged up to the halter.

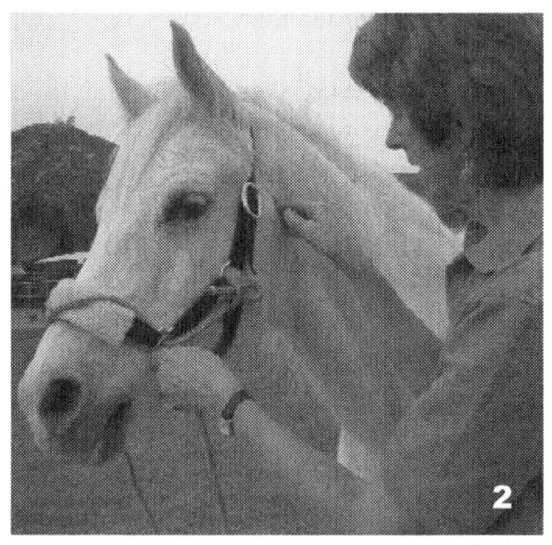

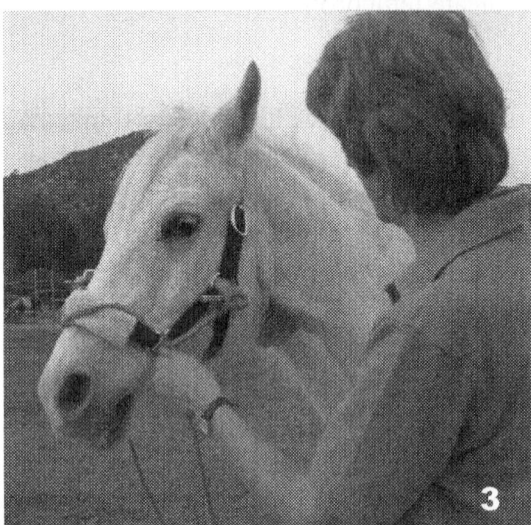

With the right hand, place your index, middle and ring fingers in the groove just below the ear behind the cheekbone and slowly delineate the groove downward following the outline of the cheekbone. Use 2 or 3 degrees of pressure.

Do this two or three times and then let the horse think about it. If there are areas that seem thicker or harder to the touch, you may have to slow down or stay in a spot for a few seconds and lighten the touch. About halfway down you may notice some thickening or hardening under your fingers. This is the area where salivary glands and lymph glands are and there is often congestion due to tension in the poll and upper neck area of the horse. *Cheek Delineation* helps release this congestion.

Connected Groundwork I: Exercises for Developing and Maintaining
Freedom of Movement and Self-Carriage
© 2004 Connected Enterprises, Inc.
By Peggy Cummings with photographs by Lynne Glazer
Call 1-800-310-2192 or visit www.connectedriding.com

Once the horse has softened in the throatlatch area, in order to remind his nervous system of its natural ability to rotate laterally at the poll, go to the midpoint of the outer line of the cheekbone as shown in the photos below. This suggests to the horse that he can rotate and easily slide his head to the left or right. The midpoint is the place that the horse's head turns with freedom. If there is release and freedom in this area, the horse will achieve more ease in releasing and bending throughout the rest of his body.

OBSERVATIONS:

As the horse releases, you may see any of the following: lowering of the head, ease in rotation of the head, licking, chewing, taking a deep breath, nostrils flaring, whiskers wiggling, eyes closing and an increase in focus. Next, take the horse for a brief walk and look for differences in the gait, such as freer movement.

When there is restriction in this area, the horse will object to the delineation. He may pull his head away, become very unfocused, back up or fidget. If you go to the midpoint and suggest rotation, the horse either will object to your fingers being there or will not rotate even when fingers are at the midpoint.

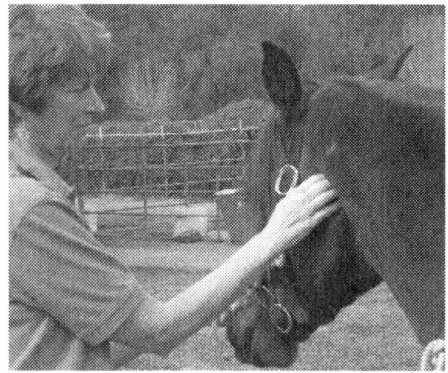

Midpoint of the cheek: When this area is free, the horse's head and neck will rotate and release at this point. If the horse is tight, he will tilt his head and resist the motion.

What happens after you try the exercise? If the horse seems to settle and focus, you are on the right track; if not, go to the other side and see what the result is. You may have to go on to another exercise. Sometimes in horses' process of releasing restrictions, they are initially unable to complete some of the exercises, but when taken for a walk or allowed time to process, they will consistently improve their movement and have a greater aptitude for learning and releasing tension or holding patterns in their bodies.

Remember to Remember
If your horse gets stuck—
Go for a walk...
Stand still for 30 seconds....
Allow your horse to process the learning...

Connected Groundwork I: Exercises for Developing and Maintaining
Freedom of Movement and Self-Carriage
© 2004 Connected Enterprises, Inc.
By Peggy Cummings with photographs by Lynne Glazer
Call 1-800-310-2192 or visit www.connectedriding.com

CATERPILLAR

PURPOSE

Caterpillar promotes telescoping of the horse's neck during movement, ensuring release of the poll, base of the neck and shoulders. This exercise helps horses stretch into contact and yield through turns.

PROCEDURE:

Stand facing the horse's neck on the left side. Hook your index or index and middle fingers of your left hand in front of the "T" junction of the halter's noseband near the lower ring (see photo at left). The purpose of hooking the fingers is to make a connection and steady the head, but use common sense and be prepared to remove your fingers quickly should your horse become startled. Another option is to snug your hand up to the halter (as shown below right) while maintaining lightness in your hand.

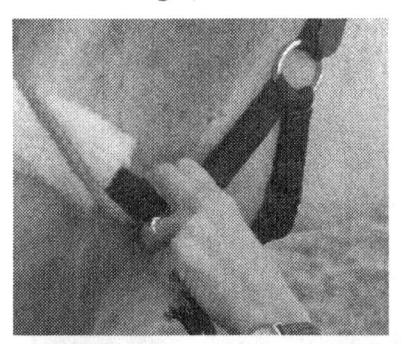

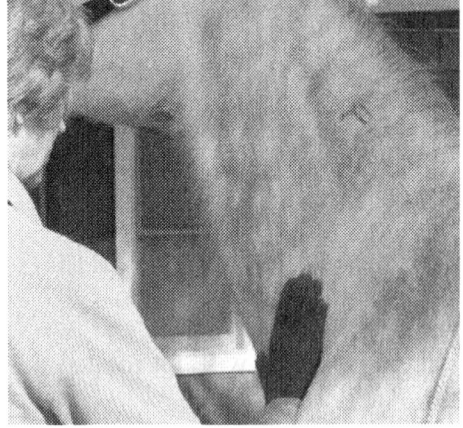

Now place your right hand at the base of the neck above the point of the shoulder. Your thumb will be on or close to the jugular groove and the rest of the fingers will be at the top ridge of the vertebrae near the base of the neck. It will feel as if you are cupping your hand around the vertebrae.

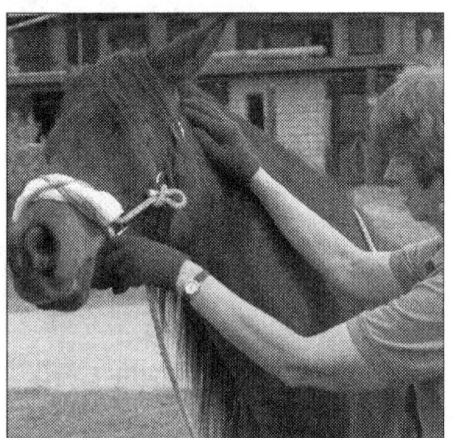

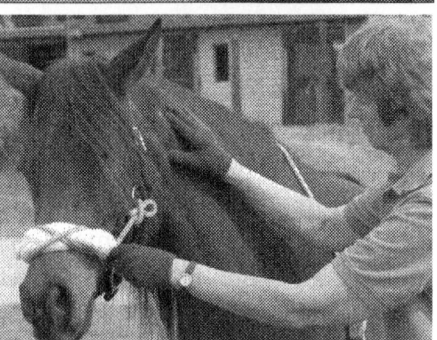

Begin the exercise at the base of the neck near the jugular groove.

First, slide up the neck toward the horse's ear using the base (heel) of your hand. Practice smooth connected movement with 2 to 4 degrees of pressure. Think of moving your hand like a caterpillar that inches up the neck, vertebra by vertebra. As the base of your hand moves toward the ears, allow your fingers to plow through the hair like a bulldozer. Finally, add the action of opening and closing your

If the horse reacts to tightness at the top of the neck; stop the exercise, take the horse for a walk, let her process and then come back and try again or move to a different exercise.

Connected Groundwork I: Exercises for Developing and Maintaining
Freedom of Movement and Self-Carriage
© 2004 Connected Enterprises, Inc.
By Peggy Cummings with photographs by Lynne Glazer
Call 1-800-310-2192 or visit www.connectedriding.com

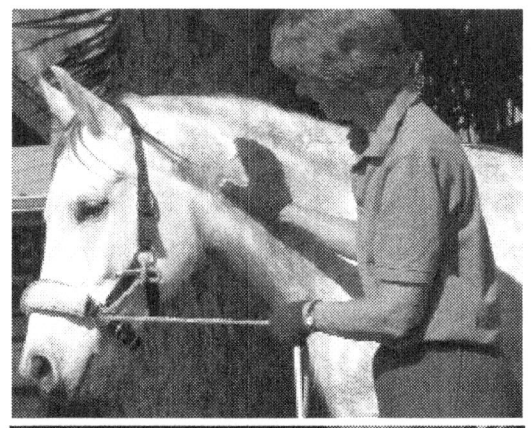

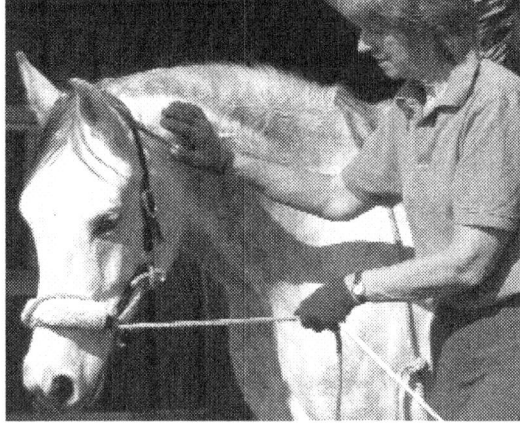

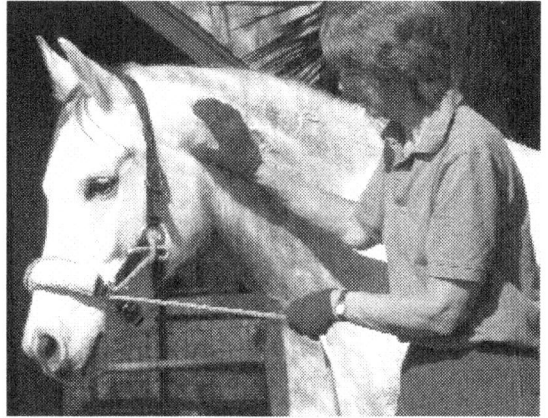

Variation: Caterpillar at the walk with one hand on the line. Note progressive lowering of head.

thumb and fingers like a clamshell as you travel up the neck. Slightly cup your hand and fingers during the movement. Repeat this exercise four to five times and if necessary, give the horse time to process in between.

OBSERVATIONS:

When the horse releases, the head lowers, the eyes soften, the mouth relaxes and the neck telescopes, the nostrils flare, and sometimes the horse takes a big breath or snorts. Oftentimes after taking a walk, horses will stand more squarely.

When the horse is tense (as shown by the bay mare in the near left photos, facing page), as you start up the neck, the head might come up or the horse may move away from you, back up or try to nip or bite. If lightening your pressure and simplifying the exercise by softly passing your hand up the neck does not release the horse's tension or gain his trust, stop doing the exercise. Take the horse for a short walk to allow time for processing, then try again, go to the other side or move on to another exercise.

To increase your awareness of your horse's reactions, ponder the following questions: Is the horse able to release his head forward and down? Does he toss his head? Does he tighten and brace against you? Is the horse able to stand still? What happens when you stop doing the exercise?

CHIN REST

PURPOSE:

Chin Rest relieves tension in the poll and upper regions of the neck. It also helps reeducate horses who go behind the vertical by allowing them to regain trust and relearn how to open their throatlatch. *Chin Rest* encourages horses to telescope and stretch down into contact.

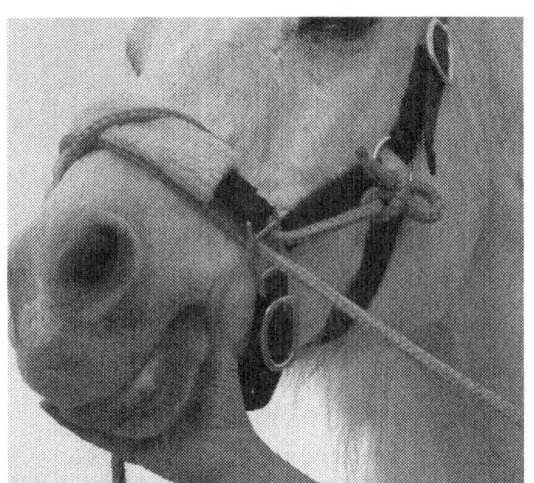

PROCEDURE:

Stand on the left side of the horse by his head, facing forward. Gently cup your right hand under the horse's chin groove and meet the weight of the head in your hand. Support the weight for 10 to 90 seconds or longer if the horse is showing signs of relaxation. Next, slowly release the weight of the head from your hand. Allow him to process for 30 to 60 seconds or longer if necessary before repeating the exercise two to four times.

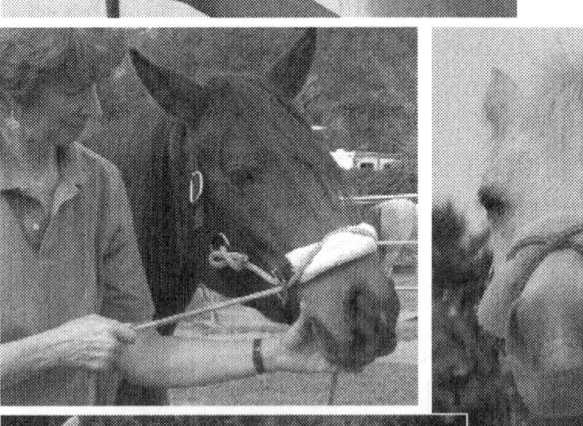

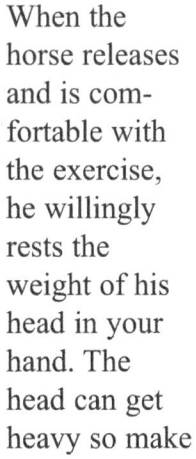

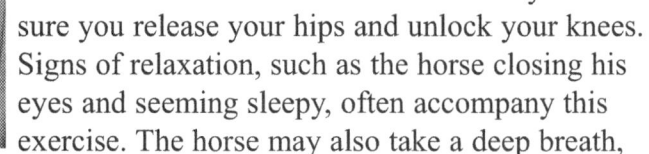

When the horse releases and is comfortable with the exercise, he willingly rests the weight of his head in your hand. The head can get heavy so make sure you release your hips and unlock your knees. Signs of relaxation, such as the horse closing his eyes and seeming sleepy, often accompany this exercise. The horse may also take a deep breath, let the nostrils flare, let out a good snort, or shake either his neck or entire body. When

---

Connected Groundwork I: Exercises for Developing and Maintaining
Freedom of Movement and Self-Carriage
© 2004 Connected Enterprises, Inc.
By Peggy Cummings with photographs by Lynne Glazer
Call 1-800-310-2192 or visit www.connectedriding.com

you slowly release the weight of the horse's head, it often drops lower than it was before, and frequently the horse will telescope and stretch his head and neck all the way to the ground.

OBSERVATIONS:
When a horse has a lot of tightness and stiffness in the neck and poll, he can react in two ways. If the horse typically raises his head in tension or transitions, in the beginning of this exercise he may not even accept contact under the chin. Or he may accept contact but not release his head so that you will be supporting ounces of weight instead of pounds. In this case, if you just barely add a few ounces of lift, often the horse will respond by beginning to let the head go. If the horse continues to back away or toss his head, then stop doing the exercise for the moment. Go for a short walk and observe whether the horse's head is lower and the walk freer, even though the horse objected to the exercise. Go back to some of the other exercises and then try again.

Chin Rest, walking. Notice how I have released my back in the top photo.

Ask yourself some of the following questions to aid you in your observations: Does the horse toss his head? Is the horse's head heavy or light? After repeating the exercise several times, note any changes in behavior. Does the horse release and stretch down when you release? Is the horse able to stand still while you do this exercise?

Remember to Remember
Never be invested in making the horse "do" any exercise. The horse is not being stubborn or disrespectful if he is not cooperating. If he is unable to perform an exercise, the horse is most likely experiencing tightness or discomfort somewhere on the body. If the tightness or discomfort continues, the horse may need some chiropractic or other therapeutic support.

Connected Groundwork I: Exercises for Developing and Maintaining
Freedom of Movement and Self-Carriage
© 2004 Connected Enterprises, Inc.
By Peggy Cummings with photographs by Lynne Glazer
Call 1-800-310-2192 or visit www.connectedriding.com

SHOULDER DELINEATION

PURPOSE:
Shoulder Delineation helps horses overcome patterns of bracing the shoulder during forward movement and turns as well as release tight back muscles. This exercise also helps horses shift their weight from side to side, from base down to base up, and from forehand to haunches.

PROCEDURE:
Stand on the horse's left side facing forward with your left hand connected to the halter or line. With your body slightly rotated and folded at the hip, place your fingers at the top of the shoulder just below the withers in front of the ridge of the scapula. With your fingers together and pointing downward, follow the groove that begins in front of the shoulder blade and slowly travel down along its edge, curving your fingers into the groove. Often, when you begin *Shoulder Delineation* at the top of the scapula, the groove will be tight. As you move downward, you will be able to delineate more deeply. Then, as you approach the point of the shoulder, the delineation again becomes more shallow. To help the horse relax and open more in this area, place your hand at the T-junction of the halter's lower ring and slowly rotate his head towards you.

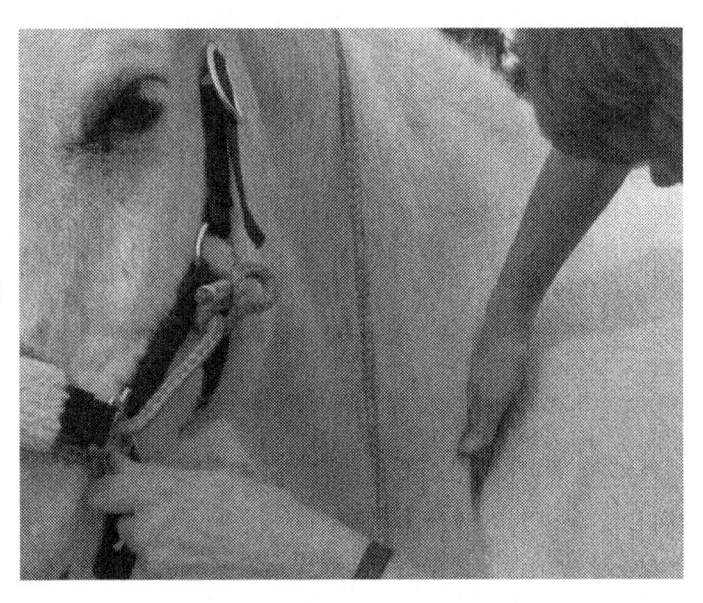

OBSERVATIONS:
As the horse releases, you will notice signs of acceptance or relaxation, and the horse may begin to lower his head and telescope his neck. Notice if one side is easier to delineate than the other.

If the horse resists your fingers tracing the groove, he may object by backing up, twitching the skin or moving away, all signs of tightness and tension. Slow the process and lighten your touch; try the other side or take the horse for a brief walk. Even though the horse objected to the exercise, always notice the quality of the horse's walk, how he comes to a stop and how he is standing. Signs of bracing or tightness are common in this area, and the groove may be nearly impenetrable to the fingers except with very young horses in whom the groove can be delineated more easily.

Connected Groundwork I: Exercises for Developing and Maintaining
Freedom of Movement and Self-Carriage
© 2004 Connected Enterprises, Inc.
By Peggy Cummings with photographs by Lynne Glazer
Call 1-800-310-2192 or visit www.connectedriding.com

SHOULDER PRESS

PURPOSE:
Shoulder Press supports the horse as he releases the shoulder and base of the neck, bends and releases the ribcage. It aids the horse in releasing habitual bracing patterns that encourage one-sidedness and crookedness. A horse needs to be able to easily yield his shoulder and bend through the ribcage—creating a "C" shape with his body—in order to initiate pushing power from the inside hind leg.

PROCEDURE:
Begin by standing on the left side facing the horse's withers. Your left hand connects with the horse's head on the line at the halter or the index and middle fingers can hook in front of the "T" junction of the halter near the lower ring.

Make a soft fist with your right hand and place it in the fleshy muscle about two to three fist lengths (depending on the size of the horse) back from the point of the shoulder. Your feet should be slightly apart, one ahead of the other. The right foot is ahead and closer to the horse if you are pressing on the left shoulder with the right hand.

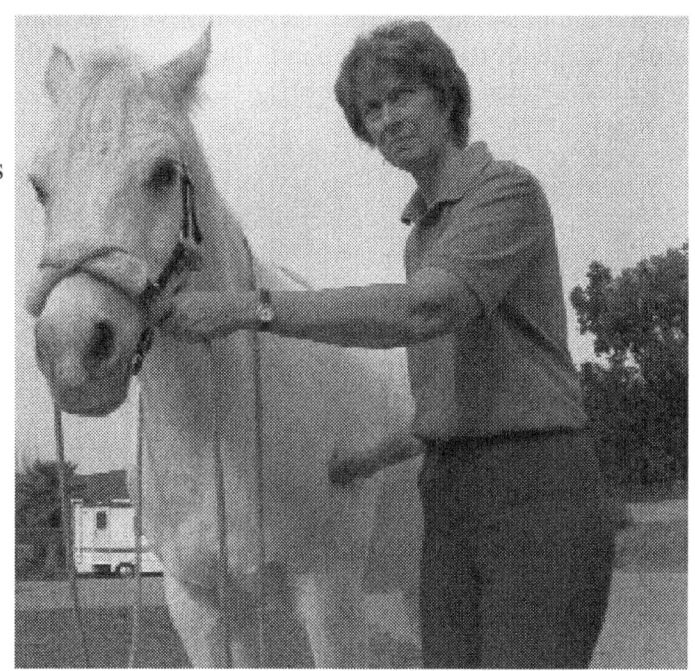

Shoulder Press: This horse is accepting my contact and processing the exercise. He is responding by shifting his weight to the outside leg, releasing the base of the neck and beginning to bend his body in a C-curve.

Begin by pressing to meet the pressure that you feel in the horse's shoulder, and notice the horse's reaction. It is very important to be sure that as you are pressing, your back, hips and knees are released, and you allow a slight rotation in your body. The rotation is to the left if pressing with the right hand.

The most important part of the exercise is the *slow release* of the pressure, as this is the time that the horse finds new ways of using himself to change habitual bracing patterns. Try this routine: Press while counting 1-2-3-4, then slowly release 1-2-3-4-5-6-7-8.

OBSERVATIONS:
As with any of the other exercises, look for signs of relaxation and that the horse's nervous system is accepting the information. Does the horse lower his

---

Connected Groundwork I: Exercises for Developing and Maintaining
Freedom of Movement and Self-Carriage
© 2004 Connected Enterprises, Inc.
By Peggy Cummings with photographs by Lynne Glazer
Call 1-800-310-2192 or visit www.connectedriding.com

head? Does he feel softer and more pliable under your fist? Does it seem to take very little pressure to shift his weight away from your fist to the outside leg?

When the horse releases, you will see his head lowering along with licking, chewing and softening under your fist and shifting weight to the outside leg.

When the horse is bracing, you will feel heaviness and no give under your hand. The horse may raise his head more and back up or move away.

A variation of *Shoulder Press*, shown below, is to maintain connection with the outside rein or line with the pressing hand. This encourages the horse to release into contact.

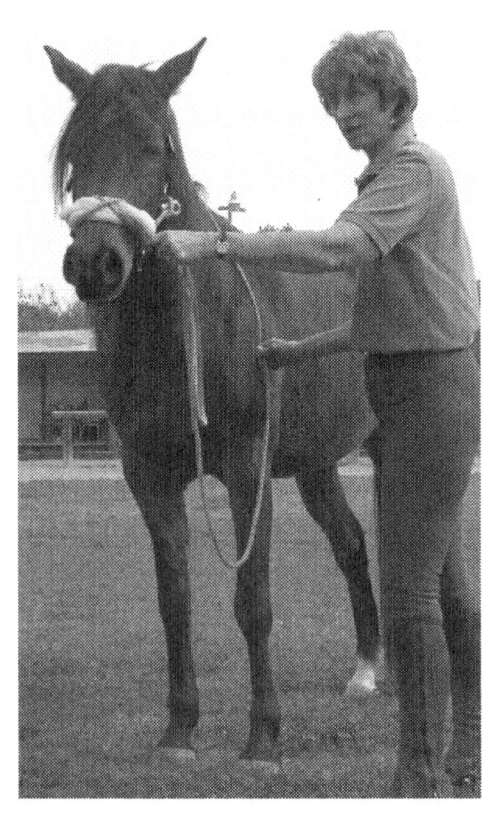

Left: Notice the additional support the horse is receiving when I maintain a connection on the outside line along with **Shoulder Press**.

Right: As I'm rotating and pressing into the mare's shoulder, she is shifting her weight and softening through the middle, creating a "C" curve through her body and releasing into connection.

Connected Groundwork I: Exercises for Developing and Maintaining Freedom of Movement and Self-Carriage
© 2004 Connected Enterprises, Inc.
By Peggy Cummings with photographs by Lynne Glazer
Call 1-800-310-2192 or visit www.connectedriding.com

HEART-GIRTH PRESS

PURPOSE:
Heart-Girth Press gives the horse freedom to release the base of the neck and ribcage. This allows him to bend through the body, initiating engagement from the inside hind leg and increasing the ease and depth of respiration.

PROCEDURE:
Stand at the horse's left side with your feet one behind the other, right foot ahead. Let your upper body bend at the hips, releasing your back, hips and knees. Place your right arm against the horse's heart girth and allow the weight of your body to press against the horse. Maintain this position for about a minute and then slowly release. Repeat two to three times and notice the changes.

Heart-Girth Press: After initially bracing and disconnecting (top), this horse accepts contact and responds by taking a deep breath, lowering the head and shifting his weight to the outside leg (right).

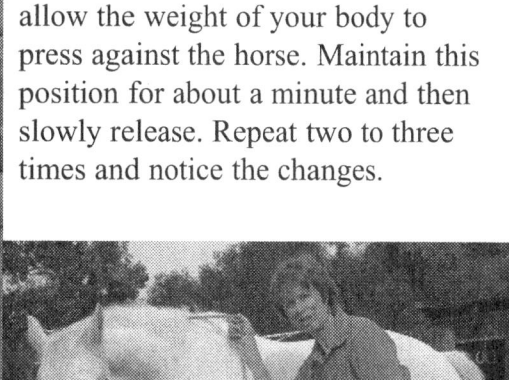

OBSERVATIONS:
As the horse releases, he softens under your arm, lowers his head and telescopes his neck. His weight shifts off the forehand as he bends through the ribcage. Lateral work comes with ease as the horse can lift his back and step under.

When a horse braces against you and resists shifting his weight, you are feeling muscle tightness and sometimes lumpy adhesions. The heart-girth area is a major bracing point in a horse's body, often due to an ill-fitting saddle or a rider's tight thighs or tense back. When this area is tight, the horse carries tension throughout his body, maintains crookedness, stays on the forehand and cannot lift his back or come through from behind during movement.

Connected Groundwork I: Exercises for Developing and Maintaining
Freedom of Movement and Self-Carriage
© 2004 Connected Enterprises, Inc.
By Peggy Cummings with photographs by Lynne Glazer
Call 1-800-310-2192 or visit www.connectedriding.com

WITHER ROCK

PURPOSE:
Wither Rock releases the base of the neck, shoulders and ribcage, encouraging horses to shift their weight from side to side freely and evenly.

PROCEDURE:
Stand at the horse's left side facing the withers. Take up a connection with the left hand on the line. Place your right foot forward and cup your right hand over the withers.

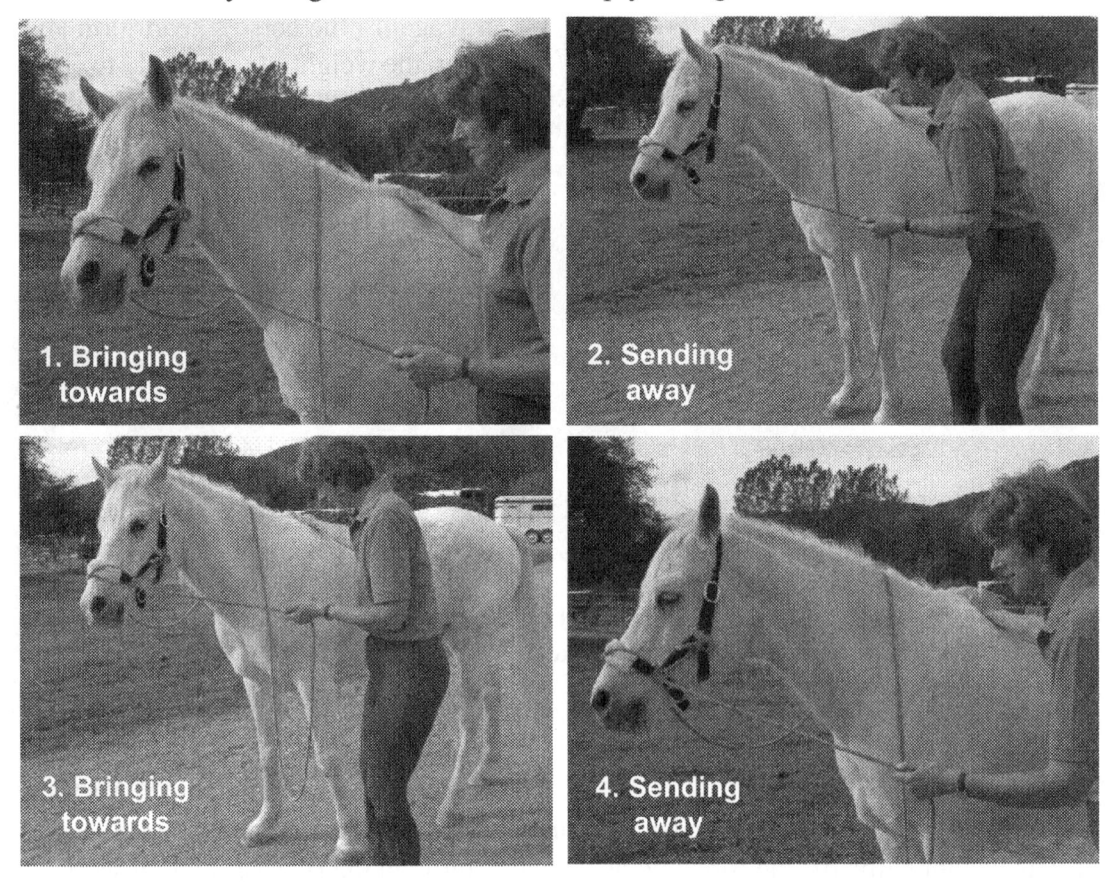

1. Bringing towards
2. Sending away
3. Bringing towards
4. Sending away

As you do the **Wither Rock** exercise, your horse may loosen up through the rib cage and as he does, he may rearrange his feet and rebalance himself as shown in **Photo 3**.

Begin a very slow movement of rocking your weight onto your left foot and bringing the withers toward you. Then, slowly release. Continue rocking your weight forward onto your right foot, and with the heel of your hand press on the withers and send his weight away from you. Slowly release. Repeat three to four times and notice the changes. When you feel the horse is integrating the learning, repeat the movement with a lighter, quicker oscillating rhythm.

Connected Groundwork I: Exercises for Developing and Maintaining
Freedom of Movement and Self-Carriage
© 2004 Connected Enterprises, Inc.
By Peggy Cummings with photographs by Lynne Glazer
Call 1-800-310-2192 or visit www.peggycummings.com

OBSERVATIONS:

When a horse releases, the head and neck immediately start lowering and telescoping. You can clearly see the horse shift his weight from side to side, and many times he will show clear signs of relaxation such as those mentioned in previous exercises. Sometimes horses will release the base of the neck, lower their heads and move forward. When a horse resists, he will either brace against the movement, back up or move away. He might also tighten and retract the base of the neck.

When you first begin the exercise, does the horse seem heavy under your hand and braced? Does the horse's head lower? Does he take deep breaths or lick and chew? Does the exercise get easier and lighter? Does his demeanor change after a couple of repetitions? Does he shift his weight to rebalance himself?

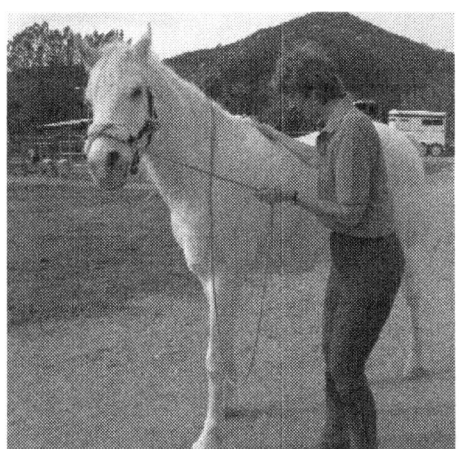

After your horse is comfortable with **Wither Rock** standing still (top), you can proceed to practice the exercise at a walk (right).

Remember to Remember
Connection originates with your neutral body posture. Every time you release any tension or bracing from your body, use your rotation instead of pulling with your hands, and engage your core abdominal muscles to stabilize and ground your body, you become a clearer, stronger support to your horse.

Connected Groundwork I: Exercises for Developing and Maintaining
Freedom of Movement and Self-Carriage
© 2004 Connected Enterprises, Inc.
By Peggy Cummings with photographs by Lynne Glazer
Call 1-800-310-2192 or visit www.connectedriding.com

SPINE ROLL

PURPOSE:
Spine Roll helps release stress along the spine and facilitates the horse's ability to lift his back.

PROCEDURE:
Stand on your horse's left side facing his spine. Holding your cupped hands about an inch apart, place your fingertips on the off side of the horse's spine with a 2 to 4 pressure. Lighten the pressure if the area seems sensitive. As in *Wither Rock*, starting with your fingertips just behind the withers, bring the horse's spine towards you, count to 3 and slowly release. Then put your thumbs together nail to nail and lay them against the spine with your fingers cupped and remaining soft. With a 2 to 4 pressure, press the spine *away* from you, count to 3 and slowly release. Repeat this procedure all the way down the horse's spine until your fingers cannot grasp the spine any longer. Take the horse for a brief walk and repeat the process on the other side. Repeat as desired.

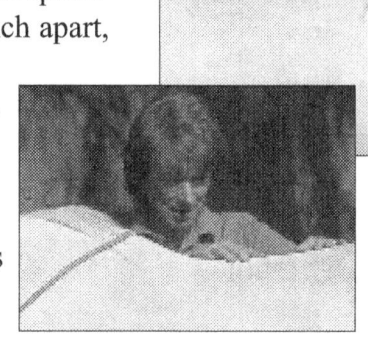

Alternate cupping hands (top) and holding thumbs together (left) to do **Spine Roll.**

OBSERVATIONS:
When a horse is sore in his back or has a lot of tension along the spine, he may react by hollowing the back in reaction to any degree of pressure. Let the horse think about it, take him for a brief walk. At this point I have often seen horses start licking and chewing and lowering their heads even if they initially had an extreme reaction. You can either try the exercise again and proceed with a light touch or do another exercise and then come back to this one. It has been my experience that a horse may show sensitivity two or three times and then be at peace, because the exercise is giving information to the nervous system about a different possibility for release. If his discomfort continues, seek the help of a chiropractor, TTEAM or other bodywork practitioner who knows how to release tension in the muscles or fascia.

When the horse releases, you will notice signs of relaxation or acceptance as you are doing the exercise or as soon as you stop. After you have finished the exercise, you may notice that the quality of the softness of the muscles along the spine has improved and/or that the horse's back has come up and that his posture is improving. You may also notice after doing this exercise that the hair is lying smoother and the skin is softer along the spine.

Connected Groundwork I: Exercises for Developing and Maintaining
Freedom of Movement and Self-Carriage
© 2004 Connected Enterprises, Inc.
By Peggy Cummings with photographs by Lynne Glazer
Call 1-800-310-2192 or visit www.connectedriding.com

SPINE RAKE

PURPOSE:
Spine Rake reminds the horse to soften and release tense muscles in the back and to raise the back. This exercise and *The Fan* (p.40) were inspired by a TTEAM exercise called *Lick of the Cow's Tongue*.

PROCEDURE:
Stand on the left side facing your horse's back. Take your right hand and beginning just behind the withers, slowly rake your hand back and forth about 12 inches on either side of the spine. Proceed all the way down to the sacrum. Repeat two to four times as needed and let the horse process or take a short walk at anytime.

Spine Rake helps soften and release tension in the back muscles. Rake your hand across the spine from the withers to the sacrum.

OBSERVATIONS:
When the horse has tension or any back soreness, he will not like the raking motion and may even act like a girthy horse. He may try to bite, kick or move away. I once had a horse buck when I gently started raking the area behind the saddle. Should your horse show any signs of reactivity, stop the exercise and let him think about it. Do another exercise and then come back to the area, and before doing any light raking, put your hand on the spine and gently and minutely oscillate the spine all the way from just behind the withers to the sacrum. The movement is with a 1 or 2 pressure, so light it is almost invisible. You want to reassure the horse that he can allow your hand in the area of discomfort. Really slowing the process down and not being invested in an end gain can result in getting the horse to release and be confident much more quickly.

When the horse releases, you will notice signs of acceptance and relaxation. You may even notice after doing the exercise that the lay of the hair is different on the horse's back and that the skin feels softer along the spine.

Connected Groundwork I: Exercises for Developing and Maintaining
Freedom of Movement and Self-Carriage
© 2004 Connected Enterprises, Inc.
By Peggy Cummings with photographs by Lynne Glazer
Call 1-800-310-2192 or visit www.connectedriding.com

THE FAN

PURPOSE:
The Fan activates movement through the ribcage by releasing patterns of bracing, especially behind the shoulder blade where the horse is often tight and the muscles atrophied due to ill-fitting saddles.

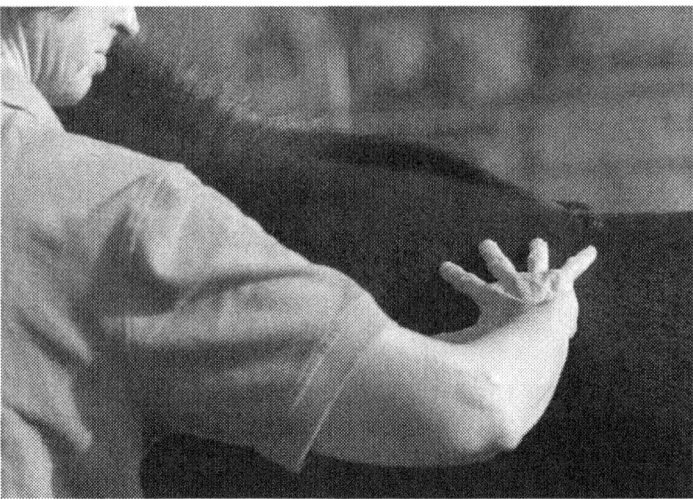

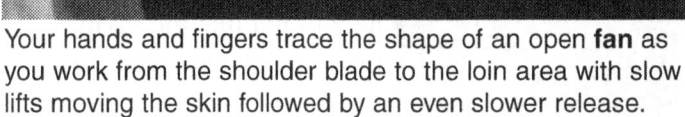

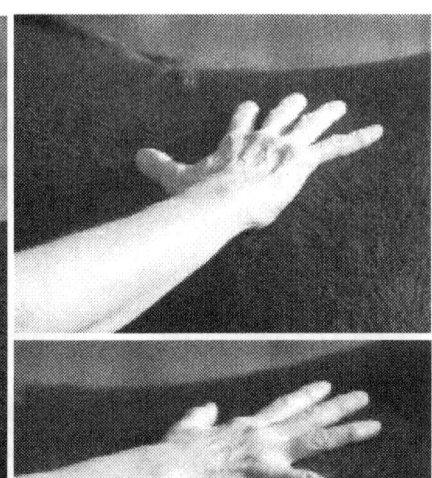

Your hands and fingers trace the shape of an open **fan** as you work from the shoulder blade to the loin area with slow lifts moving the skin followed by an even slower release.

PROCEDURE: Stand at the horse's left side facing the belly and spine. With your left hand, connect to the horse's head through the line or at the halter. Place your right hand—fingers spread in the shape of a fan—behind and below the horse's shoulder pointing towards it diagonally. Keeping your hand stationary, with a 2 or 3 pressure move the horse's skin up towards the shoulder blade. Count 1-2 and then release slowly 1-2-3-4-5-6. Move your hand to a different place and repeat two to three times. Work your way to the middle of the horse's back, and place your fingers about two to four inches below and pointing toward the spine, and repeat. Continue by placing your hand towards the loin and lift, moving the skin and using a slow release.

OBSERVATIONS: When a horse is holding tension through the back, he may not want to be touched in that area, and the skin may not move. As you begin lifting, your hand may slide because the skin is so tight underneath your hand. It may even feel like you are trying to move the top layer of fiber on wood. If you do not see a response within a few minutes, take your horse for a short walk, let him process and repeat. The change may pleasantly surprise you.

When the horse releases, you will notice more flexibility through the ribcage, the back may come up and the area behind the shoulder blade will be fuller. You may also see signs of acceptance and relaxation such as licking, chewing and head-lowering.

Connected Groundwork I: Exercises for Developing and Maintaining
Freedom of Movement and Self-Carriage
© 2004 Connected Enterprises, Inc.
By Peggy Cummings with photographs by Lynne Glazer
Call 1-800-310-2192 or visit www.connectedriding.com

THE WAVE

PURPOSE:
The Wave reminds the nervous system that sequential, reciprocal and elastic movement is possible. This exercise restores movement and releases bracing patterns so that the body can swing and move freely. The objective is to establish a reciprocal rhythm between the hands using two sequences.

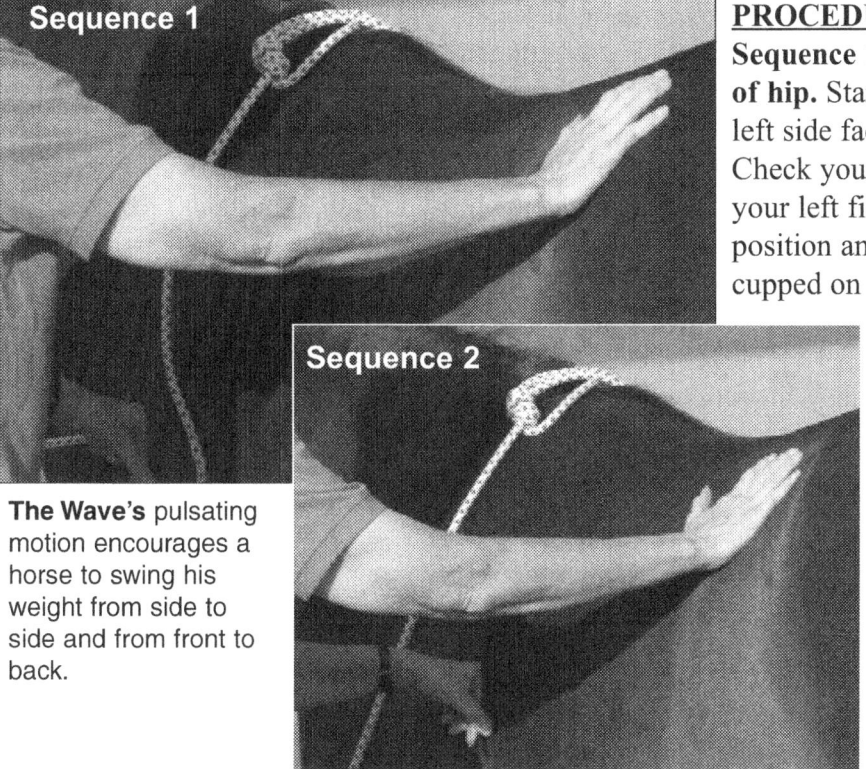

Sequence 1

Sequence 2

The Wave's pulsating motion encourages a horse to swing his weight from side to side and from front to back.

PROCEDURE:
Sequence 1: Shoulder/point of hip. Stand on the horse's left side facing the belly. Check your posture and place your left fist in *Shoulder Press* position and your right hand cupped on the point of the hip. Slightly rotate right and notice how that automatically increases the connection of your left fist on the horse's body. Press with 2 to 4 degrees of pressure as if you are asking the horse to shift his weight onto his right foreleg. Press slowly, counting 1-2; then slowly release counting 1-2-3-4-5-6. Change your rotation to the left as you press on the hip as if you are asking the horse to shift his weight onto his right hind leg. Repeat the sequence two or three times, then let the horse process. As you do the sequence a few times, notice how the wave-like motion between your hands becomes more fluid.

GENERAL RULE:
If the horse feels stiff and heavy between your hands, slow down your rotation and lighten your touch. His body needs time to learn how to release and soften without the instinctual patterns of bracing and stiffening against pressure.

Sequence 2: Heart-girth/loin. Continuing to stand on the left side of the horse, place your left fist in the heart-girth area in the middle of the horse's body as shown in the

---

Connected Groundwork I: Exercises for Developing and Maintaining
Freedom of Movement and Self-Carriage
© 2004 Connected Enterprises, Inc.
By Peggy Cummings with photographs by Lynne Glazer
Call 1-800-310-2192 or visit www.connectedriding.com

second photo. The right hand is positioned on the loin in front of the point of the hip. Repeat the exercise as in **Sequence 1**. Repeat two to three times and notice any changes in the horse's ability to move as well as any other responses to the exercise. Let the horse process. Stand and observe, go for a short walk, or both.

Sequence 3. Mix the sequences (i.e., shoulder/point of hip, heart girth/loin). Notice which sequences your horse responds to most comfortably.

OBSERVATIONS:

When the horse has tension, he may raise his head and feel heavy and rigid under your hands as you begin the exercise. It's like a sensation of dribbling a deflated basketball. Slow down the exercise and give the horse more time to process if his response is dull.

When the horse releases, you will immediately notice signs of connection or more ease in movement as you repeat the sequence. When the horse is light, you should feel like you are volleying his body back and forth between your hands. The motion feels springy, elastic and reciprocal.

What do you observe in your horse when you stop the exercise? You may notice his head lowering and he may show other signs of release such as licking, chewing, yawning, etc. You may notice the biggest difference when you take him for a short walk and suddenly feel that his movement is lighter and more animated.

> **Remember to Remember....**
> In all of the exercises presented in this book, it is very important to release *twice as slowly* as you made the initial connection.

HIP PRESS

PURPOSE:
Hip Press helps the horse to differentiate and improve lateral movement. This exercise also assists the horse in shifting his weight longitudinally.

PROCEDURE:
Stand on the left side of the horse holding the line in connection with your left hand. Cup your right hand and place it on the hipbone or point of hip. Press with 2 to 4 degrees of pressure as if you were asking the horse to step over; count 1-2, then slowly release 1-2-3-4-5-6. Repeat/process a few times. Make sure your hips, knees and lower back are released.

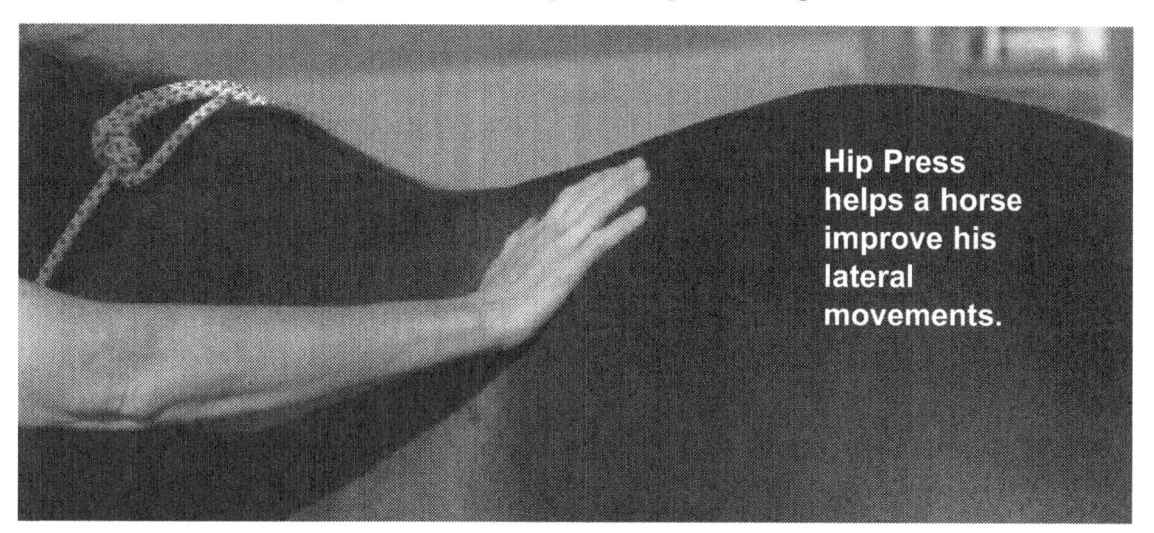

> Hip Press helps a horse improve his lateral movements.

OBSERVATIONS:
When the horse holds tension in the body, movement will be limited or absent. The horse will feel like he is bracing against you. Between repetitions, take him for a short walk, to observe even small changes; he may be in the process of releasing and regaining movement, which is the desired outcome.

When the horse releases, you will notice signs of acceptance and relaxation. The horse will lengthen his spine as you press and shift his weight sideways and backwards. As you begin the exercise, you will be giving the horse's nervous system the suggestion of movement. The second and third time you repeat the exercise (and remember to give the horse a chance to process in between each time), you may notice that the body has integrated the information and that the horse's movement is freer.

Connected Groundwork I: Exercises for Developing and Maintaining
Freedom of Movement and Self-Carriage
© 2004 Connected Enterprises, Inc.
By Peggy Cummings with photographs by Lynne Glazer
Call 1-800-310-2192 or visit www.connectedriding.com

SACRAL ROCK

PURPOSE:
Sacral Rock loosens tightness in the lumbosacral (LS) area, the part of the equine anatomy housing the most important joint for creating pushing power from behind. The LS joint allows for the swing of the walk, engagement of the hind end, and aids in transitions and straightness. It also enables the horse to rock his weight back onto his haunches. (To locate the lumbosacral joint, palpate the spine for a soft springy area near the point of the croup.)

PROCEDURE:
Before you begin this exercise, be sure the horse is comfortable with your contact on his loin, hindquarters and tail area. Stand on the horse's left side facing the hip. Place your left hand palm down on the loin with your fingers facing upwards towards the spine. Cup your right hand around the dock of the tail. As you slightly rotate to the right, your right hand brings the tail towards you as your left hand sends the loin away (top left photo).

While your right hand remains cupped over the dock of the tail, move your left hand to the off side, sliding it over the loin. The fingers of your left hand will be just on the off side of the spine. Now as you rotate slightly to the left, your left hand brings the loin towards you and your right hand sends the tail dock away (lower left photo).

Now, begin alternately rocking the horse by rotating your body right and left. This will send the spine away from you as you rock the tail towards you. Then, as you bring the spine back towards you, you will send the tail away. (photo, facing page).

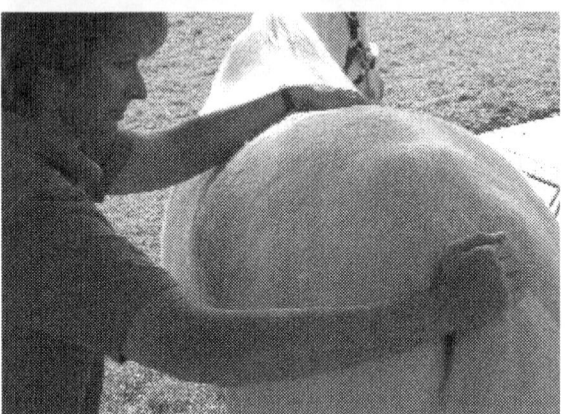

Top photo: Bringing the tail towards you and the loin away; **lower photo:** sending the tail away and the loin towards you. This exercise releases tightness through the sacral area and helps your horse engage his hindquarters.

Connected Groundwork I: Exercises for Developing and Maintaining Freedom of Movement and Self-Carriage
© 2004 Connected Enterprises, Inc.
By Peggy Cummings with photographs by Lynne Glazer
Call 1-800-310-2192 or visit www.connectedriding.com

OBSERVATIONS:

When a horse is holding tension in the lumbosacral area, you may feel little or no movement between your hands as you are doing this exercise. If this is the case, stop the exercise and let your horse process the information. Come back to the exercise later and you may find a change in his ability to move. If the horse is being reactive to the placement of your hands, try a simpler exercise such as *Tail Rock, Hip Press* or *The Wave*. If your horse is holding more tension on one side or the other you may notice that the send and toward movements feel uneven.

When the horse releases, you will notice signs of acceptance and relaxation. You may feel freer movement between your hands. The send and toward movements become more even.

Alternately rock the tail and loin with a rhythmical motion. Most horses enjoy this exercise. Be sure to work your horse from both sides.

Remember to Remember....

When a horse appears to not like an exercise or has an intense reaction to it, you will often find tightness or discomfort in the area which needs to be addressed. Often if you can go further down the body and release other parts, you can return to the tight segment to provide more support and free it up.

Connected Groundwork I: Exercises for Developing and Maintaining Freedom of Movement and Self-Carriage
© 2004 Connected Enterprises, Inc.
By Peggy Cummings with photographs by Lynne Glazer
Call 1-800-310-2192 or visit www.connectedriding.com

TAIL ROCK

PURPOSE:
Tail Rock frees the horse's movement through the spine and hindquarters and encourages his ability to rock back on the haunches.

PROCEDURE:
Make sure you are safe in approaching the horse's tail and that you can cup your hand around the tail at the dock. Standing on the left side of the horse close to the tail, place your left hand on his loin and cup your right hand over the dock of the tail. Using both hands, slowly rock the hindquarters in a back and forth rhythm initiated by your hand on the dock of the tail.

OBSERVATIONS:
If the horse is tense through the body, initially you may see no response to your oscillations. He may feel tight to your touch or clamp his tail as you place your hands on the dock. Should this occur, do different Connected Groundwork or TTEAM exercises on other areas of the body, then come back to the tail. In some horses, the tail may be quite flaccid and feel disconnected from the body.

When the horse lets in this movement, you will notice his entire body swaying from your gentle oscillations. Most horses enjoy the sensation.

Connected Groundwork I: Exercises for Developing and Maintaining
Freedom of Movement and Self-Carriage
© 2004 Connected Enterprises, Inc.
By Peggy Cummings with photographs by Lynne Glazer
Call 1-800-310-2192 or visit www.connectedriding.com

INTRODUCTION TO CONNECTED LEADING

The exercises that I have presented so far have all been shown on a horse standing still. All of the exercises, some with slight modifications, can also be done while the horse is walking. These will be covered in more detail in the next volume of the Connected Groundwork series.

To lead your horse in connection, you will need to learn the following exercises: *Tracing the Arc, Elephant's Trunk, Slide Up/Slide Out* and *Walking the S, One Hand*. *Tracing the Arc* ensures freedom in the neck as the horse bends through a curve. *Elephant's Trunk* also frees the base of the neck and ensures that changes of direction can be made with ease. *Slide Up/Slide Out* supports the horse to take a connection on the line while maintaining forward motion.

Leading in Connection, in stride, with ease: At the beginning of the session, this mare would not step over a walkway of bricks. Less than 30 minutes later, after doing standing exercises and **Walking the S, One Hand**, this was the result. Notice the lowered head and flared nostrils.

Connected Leading synchronizes you and your horse walking together. *Remember to remember* that connection originates with your neutral body posture.

Every time you release any tension or bracing from your body, use your rotation instead of pulling with your hands, and engage your core abdominal muscles to stabilize and ground your body, you become a clearer, stronger support to your horse. Therefore, in order to be leading in connection, your body is most effective when it's in "neutral".

Connected Groundwork I: Exercises for Developing and Maintaining Freedom of Movement and Self-Carriage
© 2004 Connected Enterprises, Inc.
By Peggy Cummings with photographs by Lynne Glazer
Call 1-800-310-2192 or visit www.connectedriding.com

When walking in neutral with your horse, your body moves with a gentle oscillating rhythm. This rhythm moves from your feet, through your body, and is transmitted to your horse from your hands through the lead line. When you are leading in connection, this reciprocal oscillation moves from horse to human, and human to horse. Connected Leading supports balance in horses without using force and dominance.

Connected Leading provides:

- Awareness of how to lead by supporting instead of pulling
- A way to override bracing and tension patterns in you and your horse
- A better quality walk for your horse
- More effective posture for you and your horse
- A method to strengthen your horse's pushing power and his ability to carry weight.

When you begin Connected Leading exercises, start with your hand snugged up to the halter (see photo at right). As your horse progresses through these exercises, you can lead him on a longer line and stay in connection.

Gradually the horse will begin to carry himself when there is some slack in the line (see photo at left). If the horse shows signs of disconnection—lack of focus, rushing or lacking forward motion, etc.—you can slide up on the line to the halter, *Walk an "S"*, *Slide Up/Slide Out* and reconnect with the horse to facilitate his rebalancing.

Begin with your hand snugged up to the halter...

...Later you can add some slack while maintaining connection.

Connected Groundwork I: Exercises for Developing and Maintaining Freedom of Movement and Self-Carriage
© 2004 Connected Enterprises, Inc.
By Peggy Cummings with photographs by Lynne Glazer
Call 1-800-310-2192 or visit www.connectedriding.com

TRACING THE ARC

49

PURPOSE:
Tracing the Arc enables the horse to release his poll and free up his range of motion from the base of his neck. It allows the horse to bend through his body in a "C"-curve.

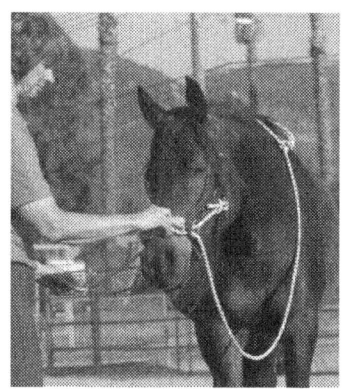

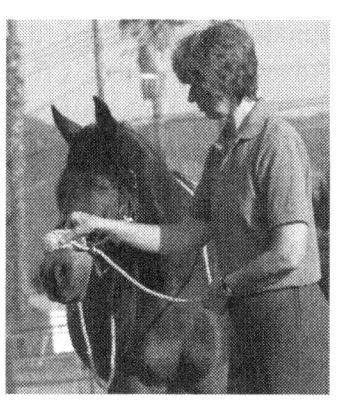

Notice how the horse progressively releases her head each time I take a step to the side. This horse is releasing well in both directions as her head lowers.

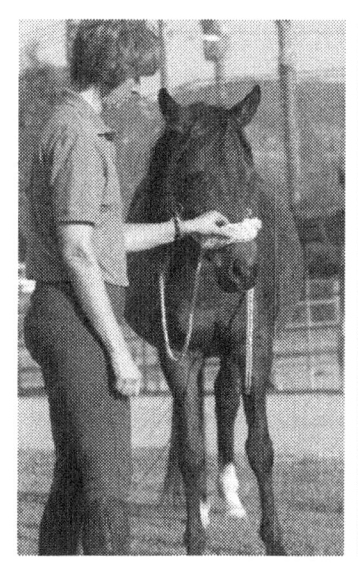

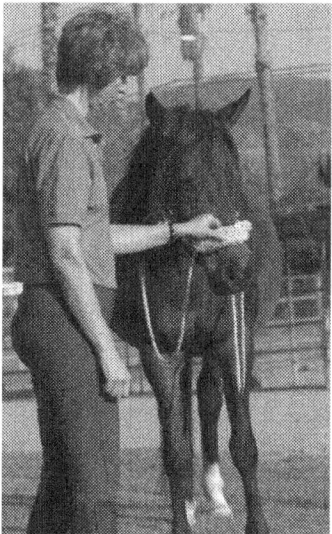

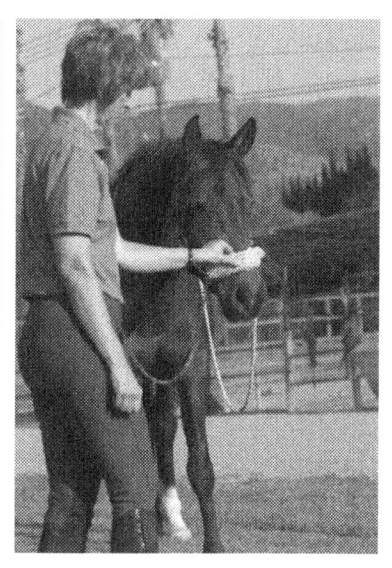

The mare is relaxed and her eye is soft as I **Trace the Arc** in the other direction. She's giving smoothly in tiny increments, signifying that all segments are releasing and bending. Some horses are unable to release in one direction and will let you know by tossing their head. Should this reaction occur, change direction, ask for less or give more time to process.

PROCEDURE:
Begin by facing the horse (you are at the center of the arc) with your index finger or index and middle fingers hooked near the middle of the noseband. Remember to soften

---

Connected Groundwork I: Exercises for Developing and Maintaining
Freedom of Movement and Self-Carriage
© 2004 Connected Enterprises, Inc.
By Peggy Cummings with photographs by Lynne Glazer
Call 1-800-310-2192 or visit www.connectedriding.com

your knees, hips and back and keep your arm light. *Your feet are stepping in an imaginary, rainbow-like arc that begins and ends from shoulder to shoulder of your horse. This arc delineates the optimal range of motion when the base of his neck is free.*

With your right hand hooked onto the halter, take one step to the left. Pause and let the horse release his head. Slowly take two or three more steps left, pausing for a release each time. When you first try this exercise, you may only be able to move a couple of steps in one direction before your horse feels stuck and unable to release. This is the time to switch your hands (i.e., from right hand to left) on the halter and step by step, move back in the other direction.

OBSERVATIONS:

When the horse is tense or braced, he will toss his head, back up, make faces, become mouthy or not want you to touch the halter. It has been my experience that when the horse does not want you near his head, there may be a problem with his teeth, the TMJ joint or the cervical vertebrae. When the horse is stiff and used to bracing on the forehand, the first time or two that you try this exercise the horse may release when you take a step and then disconnect when you take the next one. If this occurs, slow the process down further. Stop the exercise, go for a walk and come back to it or save it for another day. Return to *Cheek Press, Cheek Delineation, Caterpillar, Shoulder Delineation* and *Chin Rest* with plenty of processing time, and then try *Tracing the Arc* again.

> **Remember to Remember:**
> With *Tracing the Arc*, it is your *stepping sideways movement*, with fingers lightly connected to the halter, that directs and suggests movement to the horse's head and neck. Do not use your hand to push or pull to direct the horse. You are asking him to move from the base of his neck following the direction your steps.

When the horse progressively releases with each step, he is light in hand and focused. He is also able to curve through his body and give his head and neck with ease. Over time, as your horse releases the base of his neck, you may be able to step all the way to the end of the arc just in front of his shoulder on both sides. Your horse's range of neck motion expands with each incremental release. However, do not try to force the motion by taking steps without his neck releasing.

TRACING THE ARC AT THE WALK

When this exercise is done while walking, it becomes *Walking the S, One Hand* (see p. 55).

ELEPHANT'S TRUNK

PURPOSE:
Elephant's Trunk helps the horse release at the base of his neck. The goal of this exercise is for the horse's head and neck to move smoothly and evenly as a unit in both directions.

PROCEDURE:
Stand at the horse's head on his left side. Slide your right hand up snugly to the halter and take the slack out of the line. The horse's head must be facing forward when beginning this exercise. Gently and slowly send his head away from you. As you can see in the photos on p.52, I start the exercise with the horse's head close to my body. By opening my arm at my elbow, I send the horse's head away from me. *This is a very slow movement.* Then slowly bring the horse's head and neck back to the starting position by stretching your elbow back to your side.

Take time to notice the smoothness of the movement. See how far you can go without the horse disconnecting—losing focus, moving a foot, or raising, tossing or cocking his head. If the horse disconnects, stop the exercise for a few seconds. When you resume the exercise, slow down the process or change the direction of movement. You can also stop the exercise and give the horse time to integrate the information.

OBSERVATIONS:
Some horses, in the beginning of the exercise, appear focused and comfortable. Then, all of a sudden, the horse suddenly starts tossing his head, backing up, moving forward or losing focus. The horse may even act grouchy. These kinds of reactions indicate that the horse is bracing, has tension or is uncomfortable somewhere in his body. If you stop the exercise and go for a walk, you may notice signs of relaxation. Sometimes when you ask the horse to do the exercise the next day, his signs of discomfort diminish. You may also be pleasantly surprised to find your horse doing this exercise with ease and enjoyment!

When the horse releases you may immediately notice signs of relaxation, such as nostrils flaring, licking, chewing, or eyes closing. The horse may also quietly focus throughout the exercise. When you take the horse for a walk, his head may be lower or his transitions into the walk and halt are lighter. You may also notice that the stride of his walk has improved.

See photos on next page.

Connected Groundwork I: Exercises for Developing and Maintaining
Freedom of Movement and Self-Carriage
© 2004 Connected Enterprises, Inc.
By Peggy Cummings with photographs by Lynne Glazer
Call 1-800-310-2192 or visit www.connectedriding.com

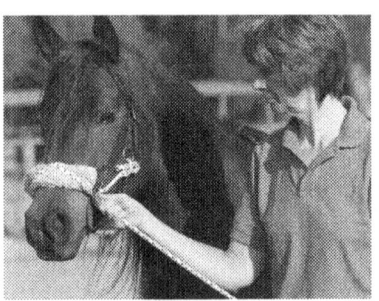

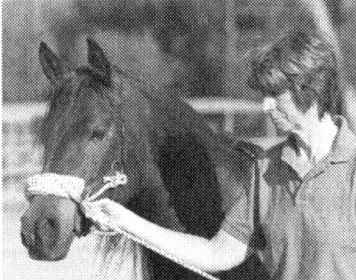

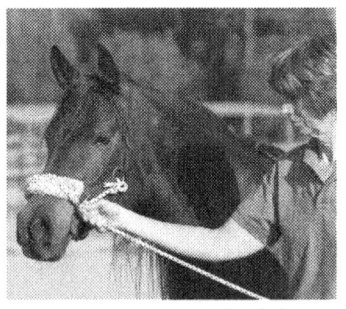

Beginning Elephant's Trunk: I very slowly send the horse's head away in a smooth, light, continuous movement. The contact in my hand is light and my arm is thinking "up".

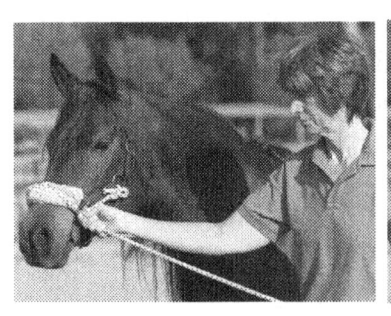

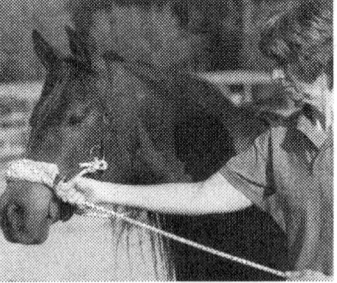

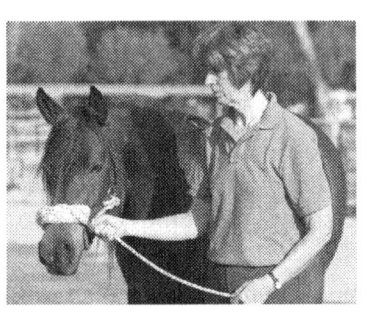

In the middle photo, the mare's head is the furthest point away. As I bring her head back towards me, she releases the base of neck and lowers her head with a mellower expression.

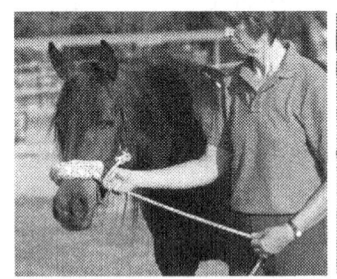

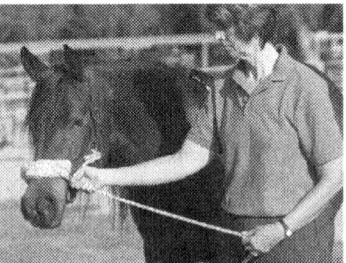

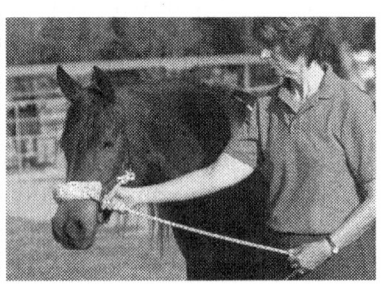

I send her head away once more. The goal of this exercise is to maintain the smoothness of the movement and the focus of the horse. You may notice other signs of relaxation, such as flared nostrils, licking or chewing or eyes closing as your horse becomes more present.

Elephant's Trunk, like many of the Connected Groundwork exercises in this book, helps horses—
- Lower the head
- Release tension in the neck
- Stop bracing and begin focusing
- Stand squarely and in balance on all four feet
- Even out the movement of the neck of a horse that is one-sided
- Maintain a rhythm and build confidence.

Connected Groundwork I: Exercises for Developing and Maintaining Freedom of Movement and Self-Carriage
© 2004 Connected Enterprises, Inc.
By Peggy Cummings with photographs by Lynne Glazer
Call 1-800-310-2192 or visit www.connectedriding.com

SLIDE UP/SLIDE OUT

PURPOSE:
Slide Up/Slide Out promotes the natural rotation and oscillation of the poll. It encourages the horse to telescope into contact by releasing the base of his neck and softening his poll. This exercise on the line shows a horse how to reciprocate in connection and helps him learn to shift his weight.

PROCEDURE:
Stand at your horse's left side. Loop and gather the line in your left hand. Leave no more than two feet of line between your left hand and the halter. It is the job of your left elbow to support a stretchy connection on the line. Your right hand is free to slide up the line to the halter and then to slide back out on the line.

Keep your left elbow bent in riding position and hold the excess line softly in your left hand. Now, slightly stretch back with your left elbow and slowly run your right hand up the line to the halter. As you slide up the line, notice how you are creating an equal and opposing force between your left elbow and right hand. When you slide all the way up the line, make a connection at the halter by adding a few ounces of pressure, as if you were sending the horse's head away. Pause and allow the horse time to process this feeling before sliding out slowly. When you slide out on the line, "own" your elbow and lighten your forearm by "thinking up", so that you have a straight line of connection between your elbow and the horse's halter. Continue to slide up and slide out several times. Then take the horse for a walk.

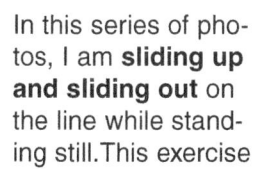

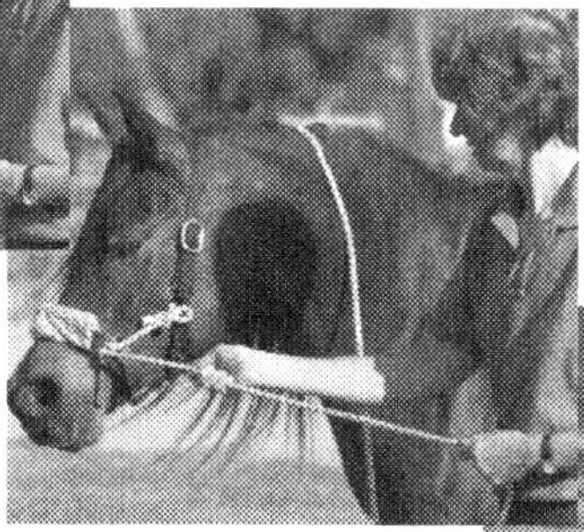

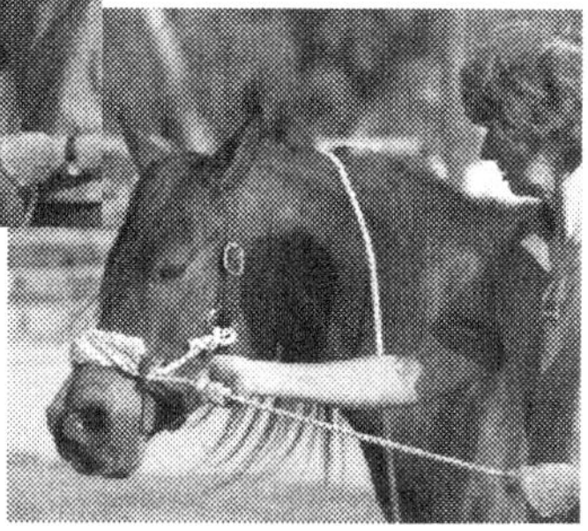

In this series of photos, I am **sliding up and sliding out** on the line while standing still. This exercise teaches the horse to stay where he is in comfort. Every time you make a connection to the halter and slide out, you will encourage head-lowering, softening at the poll and maintaining connection on the line.

OBSERVATIONS:
When the horse shows resistance, he may raise his head or not stand still. Another form of disconnection can occur when you slide out on the line and the horse starts to bring

---

Connected Groundwork I: Exercises for Developing and Maintaining
Freedom of Movement and Self-Carriage
© 2004 Connected Enterprises, Inc.
By Peggy Cummings with photographs by Lynne Glazer
Call 1-800-310-2192 or visit www.connectedriding.com

his head towards you, making it difficult to maintain connection. If this happens, slide up the line again as the horse learns to maintain connection.

When your horse releases, he may lower his head and show other signs of release. When you slide all the way up the line, make a connection and send the horse's head away, he may shift his weight. He will also be able to stay connected to the line.

COMBING THE LINE

PURPOSE:
Combing the Line is a variation of the *Slide Up/Slide Out* exercise. It supports the horse to release his poll and helps the handler avoid pulling on the horse's head. *Combing the Line* also is used to soothe and refocus horses.

PROCEDURE:
As before, take up a connection on the line with your left hand and elbow. Place your right hand on the line close to the halter and slide your right hand out about 12 to 18 inches. Now your right hand and elbow have connection on the line. Next, place your left hand on the line close to the halter and slide out. Continue sliding one hand and then the other. At no time should there be slack in the line. While combing the line, stay in neutral pelvis, lighten your arms and own your elbows.

OBSERVATIONS:
Horses always seem soothed by this exercise. They generally lower their heads, start licking and chewing, and become soft in their eyes.

WALKING THE S, ONE HAND

PURPOSE:

Walking the S, One Hand warms up the muscles of self-carriage. It encourages the horse to release stiffness from his body and to readily shift his weight while walking and changing direction. As the horse releases and shifts his weight, both sides of his body become more supple, minimizing his natural tendency to be one-sided. This serpentine-like motion will also help you assess your horse's energy and flexibility on that particular day.

PROCEDURE:

Stand at your horse's head on the left side. Slide your right hand up the line to the halter so there is no slack between your hand and the halter. Another option is to hook your index finger on the noseband as shown in the pictures of *Tracing the Arc* on p. 49. Remember to stay in neutral pelvis by keeping your back soft, your elbows bent and your arms and fingers relaxed.

The S starts with you rotating right and sending the horse away from you as you walk. In the beginning make the S loop very shallow. Walk four or five steps to the right without making too much of a curve and then slowly rotate left and take four or five steps to the left. *(This is a continuous movement. You must continue walking throughout the exercise.)* After changing your rotation and direction two or three times, walk off in a straight line and observe your horse closely.

If the horse can do the shallow S loops with ease and continues releasing while walking in a straight line, then start making deeper S loops.

Top: Start out walking with the horse moving *away* from the side the handler is on. You are looking for the horse to let go of his head in order to move his feet and release the inside shoulder, which gives him room to move.

Below: As you change the direction of your shallow serpentine to your left, make sure the horse's head is light in your hand. If it feels heavy or sticky, immediately send him away to the other side or return to **Slide Up/Slide Out.**

Connected Groundwork I: Exercises for Developing and Maintaining Freedom of Movement and Self-Carriage
© 2004 Connected Enterprises, Inc.
By Peggy Cummings with photographs by Lynne Glazer
Call 1-800-310-2192 or visit www.connectedriding.com

As you walk to the right increase your rotation. Walk slightly ahead of the horse's head in order to make a deeper curve. After four or five steps change your direction by slowly rotating your body left. Continue walking another four or five steps. Because of your increased rotation, you may need to step backwards and slightly away from the horse, giving him room to make the turn. When the horse's head is pointing towards you, change direction to the right by walking forward past his head, rotate right, and continue walking. This particular exercise takes practice.

There is something stuck if the horse is tilting the head. Should this occur, change what you're doing or allow the horse more time to process.

It is essential that your connection with the horse stays light, and you pay attention to your posture, especially if your horse is stiff and feeling heavy. If you or the horse have difficulties with this exercise go back to the shallow S loops.

OBSERVATIONS:
When the horse is stiff he may toss his head, wring his tail, stop forward movement when changing directions, back up as you ask him to move forward on a curve, or not want to move at all while you are at his head. If the horse shows signs of anger, such as pinning his ears or wanting to bite, he may have issues with his teeth, TMJ and/or spinal misalignment.

When the horse releases, the changes of direction become more fluid. When walking straight after several S loops you may notice the horse lowering his head, licking and chewing. The swing of the horse's walk will improve and he pushes more with his hind legs. The halt-walk transition will also become lighter.

A horse may move freely and release in one direction, but be very heavy or tighten in the other direction. To help the horse even out both sides, continue with the shallow S loops, but do fewer to the heavy or tight side.

> **Remember to Remember...**
> The rotation of your body suggests movement in a particular direction to the horse. Pushing or pulling with your arm does not initiate movement.

The TTouch™ Pressure Scale

For many years, TTEAM practitioners have taught the TTouch pressure scale from 1 to 10 by using contact with the eyelid as a measure of 1. However, for those wearing contacts, that does not work so well, and over the years they found that touching the soft tissue directly under the eye was easier for many people. Robyn Hood discovered that a broader range of pressure is possible using the cheekbone to establish the scale.

To learn the measure of each number, begin with the lightest pressure—using 1 as a baseline. First, bring your right hand up to your face, supporting your bent right elbow snugly against your body with your other hand. (Reverse if you are left-handed.) Then, placing your thumb against your cheek in order to steady your hand, put the tip of your middle finger just below your eye socket, and push the skin in a circle with the lightest possible contact—so you can feel only tissue with no hint of bone underneath–and just enough contact that you do not slide over the skin. This is a 1 pressure.

Next, on the fleshy part of the your forearm, between your wrist and your elbow, place your curved finger on top of the arm with your thumb on the underside so you hold the arm between the fingers and thumb. Make a circle using the same minimal possible contact as you did on your cheekbone. Observe how little indentation you make in the skin.

Register the feeling of this "1" pressure in your mind. If you wonder how such a light pressure can possibly be effective, remember, the intention is to affect the nervous system and the cells rather than the muscles themselves.

To identify a "3" pressure, repeat the process, but this time push the skin in a circle with enough pressure that you feel the top of the cheekbone clearly without pushing hard. Retaining the sensorial memory of that pressure, return to your forearm and compare this slightly increased pressure to the 1 pressure. Note the difference in indentation in your skin between the 1 and 3 pressure, and the difference in the feeling. Now go back to your cheekbone and make a circle pressing firmly on the bone itself. Take that feeling back to your forearm and you have a 6.

The indentation on your forearm will be twice as deep into the muscle with a 6 pressure. If a pressure heavier than a 6 is done with the pads of the fingers it can cause both "doer" and "do-ee" to feel discomfort and hold the breath. When working on a heavily muscled horse, making a circle with a 4 pressure and then "sponging" into the middle of the circle will help release tight muscles and increase circulation. For further information about TTouch and pressure, see any of Linda Tellington-Jones' books about TTEAM and TTouch for horses and other animals, visit their website at *www.ttouch.com* or contact the TTEAM Training office in Santa Fe, NM at 800-854-TEAM.

Connected Groundwork I: Exercises for Developing and Maintaining
Freedom of Movement and Self-Carriage
© 2004 Connected Enterprises, Inc.
By Peggy Cummings with photographs by Lynne Glazer
Call 1-800-310-2192 or visit www.connectedriding.com

GLOSSARY

Breathing from your belly (abdominal breathing). The most efficient way to maximize air intake into the lungs. When inhaling, the diaphragm is pulled down; the abdomen expands and the lungs fill with air. This action expands the ribcage in all directions, and it is felt all the way into the armpits and the lower back fills. This breathing pattern is easiest when the body is in neutral pelvis.

Bracing. Bracing is created in horse and human when muscles rigidly tighten and joints lock against movement while standing or moving.

False frame (forced frame). A human-made phenomenon created by force and bracing patterns of the rider/handler. False frame occurs when a horse travels with his head "held" by the rider/handler's hands so the poll is not allowed to release freely with each stride. When ridden this way, the horse's back and sides are also squeezed and braced against the rider's body. The base of the neck and withers stay down, limiting range of motion so the hind legs cannot track up or come under and the back cannot lift. In this posture, the horse cannot carry himself or a rider in self-carriage because he remains braced on the forehand.

Neutral pelvis. The place where the pelvis is neither tipped forward or backward; where the pelvis is resting on the middle of the seatbones (ischial tuberosity) when sitting. If the back is arched and the chest slightly lifted, the pelvis is tipped forward. Likewise, if the back is slumped and the chest slightly collapsed, the pelvis is tipped backward.

When the pelvis is in neutral, the upper body "buoys" itself, automatically rebalancing the body with each stride when walking or riding. In this position, each hip joint is free to move, allowing each leg to move independently. When sitting or standing in neutral, the body is most stable, strong and free so the limbs can be used effectively without restriction. This is the place of self-carriage in humans.

Horses rely on stability and balance from the rider/handler's body to give them support and clear communication. If you are not in neutral, the horse has to compensate for the imbalance and instability by bracing or counterbalancing. For a detailed explanation of how to find neutral pelvis, see *Connected Riding®: Exercises for Riders*.

Opening the ribcage. During abdominal "belly" breathing, as the sternum and the sacrum move away from each other, the sternum moves forward and up while the sacrum moves backward and down, allowing the back to lengthen and the ribcage to expand.

Owning your elbows. An almost invisible movement of the elbows stretching backwards to keep the slack out of the reins without tensing or bracing the body. It is this continuous reciprocal process that maintains the rider/handler's dynamic arm connection to the horse's head or mouth through the reins or line.

Connected Groundwork I: Exercises for Developing and Maintaining
Freedom of Movement and Self-Carriage
© 2004 Connected Enterprises, Inc.
By Peggy Cummings with photographs by Lynne Glazer
Call 1-800-310-2192 or visit www.connectedriding.com

Owning your elbows engages the muscles at the back of the upper arm in a soft isometric contact that is continually readjusted to maintain supportive rein contact. This is only achieved when the body is in neutral pelvis, which allows the core muscles of the body to spontaneously engage in response to the amount of support the horse needs at any given moment. It is because you are in neutral that your horse feels your rein contact (Owning Your Elbows) as supporting rather than pulling.

Plumb line. The "true vertical" line perpendicular to the ground. Just like horses, riders can be ahead, behind or "on the vertical." In most instances, however, humans are behind the vertical whether riding or standing. When a rider/handler is standing or sitting in neutral pelvis and breathing abdominally, the body has the ability to freely buoy minutely back and forth across this imaginary "plumb" line, which then passes through the ear, shoulder, hip and ankle. This buoying motion is a minute rebalancing movement (like a buoy on a wave) of the upper body over the hips. When a horse feels this rebalancing from the rider/handler's body, it supports him to buoy and rebalance too.

Rotation. Movement used by the rider/handler for making turns, changing direction, moving laterally and creating bend and straightness in the horse during riding and groundwork. Imagine the upper torso turning from deep inside the core just below the sternum. This spiral movement leverages the rider/handler's core strength. This increased strength directs the horse's movements and supports the horse to rebalance.

To ensure rotating instead of twisting, the body must be in neutral pelvis with the lower back full and soft. There is no tightening of the spine or ribcage. During rotation, the shoulders and hips remain parallel to the ground and not tipping. Rotating in neutral allows independent movement of both sides of the body.

Self-carriage (round, collected). This occurs in movement when the horse is continuously releasing at the poll, lifting his withers and the base of the neck, pushing with both hind legs and freely rebalancing himself during each stride. The horse is then able to shift his weight from front to back, back to front, from side to side and from down to up in a dynamic process.

As the horse moves, energy is generated as the push of the hind legs comes up through the horse and rider's bodies. This energy travels up through the rider to the front of the horse and then back through the rider to the hind end of the horse. It is a continuous cycle of rebalancing and reciprocity of motion and energy. As the ability to self-carry is developed, the horse is able to maintain balance and freedom for longer periods of time and the adjustments required to maintain this posture become minimal.

Telescoping the neck. In movement, the horse releases at the poll and expands his neck out and forward from the base as it moves upward. When a horse "sucks back", the base of the neck is down, the neck is contracted and compressed and the movement in the poll is constricted.

Connected Groundwork I: Exercises for Developing and Maintaining
Freedom of Movement and Self-Carriage
© 2004 Connected Enterprises, Inc.
By Peggy Cummings with photographs by Lynne Glazer
Call 1-800-310-2192 or visit www.connectedriding.com

QUICK REFERENCE GUIDE

These Connected Groundwork exercises help horses tune in when they exhibit the following common issues. We suggest, however, that you experiment with all of the exercises presented in this book to find what works best for your horse.

Difficulty changing direction
Caterpillar, Tracing the Arc, Elephant's Trunk, Cheek Press, Cheek Delineation, Walking the S, One Hand

Sticky in transitions
Caterpillar, Wither Rock, Heart-Girth Press, Hip Press, Sacral Rock, Slide Up/Slide Out

Sucking back
Caterpillar, Wither Rock, Shoulder Delineation, Heart-Girth Press, Elephant's Trunk, Slide Up/Slide Out

Behind the vertical
Caterpillar, Chin Rest, Cheek Delineation, Cheek Press, Elephant's Trunk, Slide Up/Slide Out

High head, hollow back
Caterpillar, Shoulder Delineation, Wither Rock, Cheek Press, Elephant's Trunk, The Wave

Falling in or out
Wither Rock, Shoulder Press, Cheek Press, Shoulder Delineation, Heart-Girth Press, The Fan

Cinchy/girthy
Heart-Girth Press, Shoulder Press, Spine Rake, Spine Roll, The Fan, The Wave

Leaning while standing (for farrier, etc.)
Wither Rock, Shoulder Delineation, Caterpillar, Elephant's Trunk, Shoulder Press, Sacral Rock

Trouble with trailer loading
Heart-Girth Press, Wither Rock, Shoulder Delineation, Caterpillar, Hip Press, Cheek Press, Walking the S, One Hand

Pulling back
Slide Up/Slide Out, Combing the Line, Shoulder Delineation, Chin Rest, Caterpillar, Walking the S, One Hand

Difficulty Stopping
Caterpillar, Shoulder Press, Shoulder Delineation, Tracing the Arc, Elephant's Trunk, Walking the S, One Hand

Rushing/Barging
Cheek Press, Caterpillar, Shoulder Delineation, Slide Up/Slide Out, Elephant's Trunk, Combing the Line

Trouble Standing Still
Combing the Line, Caterpillar, Shoulder Delineation, The Wave, Elephant's Trunk, Walking the S, One Hand

Kicking
Spine Rake, Spine Roll, Hip Press, The Fan, Sacral Rock, Tail Rock

Stumbling
Caterpillar, Shoulder Delineation, Wither Rock, Heart-Girth Press, The Wave, Sacral Rock, Walking the S, One Hand

Bucking
Caterpillar, Shoulder Delineation, Shoulder Press, Heart-Girth Press, Spine Roll, Spine Rake, Walking S, One Hand

Connected Groundwork I: Exercises for Developing and Maintaining Freedom of Movement and Self-Carriage
© 2004 Connected Enterprises, Inc.
By Peggy Cummings with photographs by Lynne Glazer
Call 1-800-310-2192 or visit www.connectedriding.com

RESOURCES AND RECOMMENDED READING

Books by Peggy Cummings

Connected Riding®: An Introduction, by Peggy Cummings with Diana Deterding, illustrations by Nancy Camp; Primedia Equine Group, 1999

Keys to Connection, Connected Riding Exercises for Riders, by Peggy Cummings with illustrations by Nancy Camp, Connected Riding Enterprises, Inc., 2003

Other Books

Improve Your Horse's Well-Being: A Step-by-Step Guide to TTouch and TTEAM Training, by Linda Tellington-Jones, Trafalgar Square Publishing, 1999

The Horse's Muscles in Motion, by Sara Wyche; Trafalgar Square Publishing, 2003

To order Peggy Cummings' books and equipment, including the Connected Groundwork halter and lines, call 800/310-2192 or visit
www.connectedriding.com
To order Linda Tellington-Jones' books and TTEAM equipment, call 800-854-TEAM or visit *www.ttouch.com*
Trafalgar Square toll-free order line: 800-423-4525

A word from Peggy Cummings.....

It is with joy that I share these exercises with you and your horse. Over the past 30 years, these exercises have alleviated stress, repatterned the musculature and restored freedom of movement in thousands of horses.

When I began this work, I had no idea such simple principles could facilitate such profound and lasting change. Please remember—restoring movement and changing postural habits is a gradual process. Honor yourself and your horse as you explore *Connected Groundwork.*

Peggy

Connected Groundwork I: Exercises for Developing and Maintaining Freedom of Movement and Self-Carriage
© 2004 Connected Enterprises, Inc.
By Peggy Cummings with photographs by Lynne Glazer
Call 1-800-310-2192 or visit www.connectedriding.com

CPSIA information can be obtained at www.ICGtesting.com
Printed in the USA
LVOW03s0222050514

384436LV00001B/11/A